Much Ado About Nothing

WITHDRAWN

EDITED AND RENDERED INTO MODERN ENGLISH BY
Christina Lacie, M.A.

INTRODUCTORY MATERIAL BY
Gayle Holste, M.A.

All inquiries should be addressed to:
Barron's Educational Series, Inc.
250 Wireless Boulevard
Hauppauge, NY 11788
www.barronseduc.com

ISBN-13: 978-0-7641-4178-2
ISBN-10: 0-7641-4178-3

Library of Congress Catalog Card No. 2008030043

Library of Congress Cataloging-in-Publication Data

Shakespeare, William, 1564–1616.
   Much ado about nothing / edited and rendered into modern English by Christina Lacie.
      p.   cm.—(Shakespeare made easy)
   ISBN-13: 978-0-7641-4178-2
   ISBN-10: 0-7641-4178-3
   1. Rejection (Psychology)—Drama. 2. Messina (Italy)—Drama.
3. Conspiracies—Drama. 4. Courtship—Drama. 5. Shakespeare, William, 1564–1616. Much ado about nothing. 6. Shakespeare, William, 1564–1616—Criticism and interpretation. I. Lacie, Christina. II. Title.

   PR2828.A2L33   2009
   822.3'3—dc22   2008030043

PRINTED IN THE UNITED STATES OF AMERICA

9 8 7 6 5 4 3 2

Contents

Introduction

Shakespeare Made Easy is designed to help those who struggle with Shakespeare's language read his plays with greater ease and comprehension. William Shakespeare wrote his plays to appeal to a wide audience, but in the approximately four hundred years since the plays were written, the English language has undergone significant changes. Consequently, although Shakespeare is regarded by many as the greatest playwright in the English language, readers often find the language barrier insurmountable. Even though it is possible, with practice, to read the plays in the original language, many find the task too difficult and give up either in disgust or despair. Footnotes are helpful, but they can interrupt the flow of the language, and many readers become so discouraged with having to refer to footnotes that they simply give up.

Shakespeare Made Easy offers a helping hand not only to those who want to get better acquainted with Shakespeare's plays for their own sake but also to those who are required to study the plays but find the task of deciphering the language overwhelming. Of course, there is no substitute for reading and studying the plays themselves in Shakespeare's own words. The unmatched beauty of the language can never be duplicated, but the modern version will assist the reader in distinguishing between the characters and in understanding what is happening in the play.

There are a number of possible ways to use *Shakespeare Made Easy*. One option is to read the play in the original language, referring to the modern version only when necessary. Another possibility is to read the entire play in the modern version to know what is going on and then to read the original with this knowledge firmly in mind. The bracketed notations concerning the ways in which lines may be spoken by an actor—although giving only one of the possible interpretations—can be especially helpful. If the reader plans to view a filmed version of the play, reading the modern version in advance can help overcome the difficulty of trying to understand the spoken language, as well.

Whichever method you use, *Shakespeare Made Easy* will prove a valuable resource for your study of the play. It is not intended as a substitute for the original play, since even the most careful "translation" of the text will lose certain aspects such as poetic meter, alliteration, and verbal humor.

Whether you are studying the play for a class or reading it for enjoyment or to increase your acquaintance with Shakespeare's works, the Activities section at the end of the book will be helpful in pointing out themes or issues that may have escaped your notice as you read. If you need to write a paper about this play, this section will help you generate topic ideas. It will also help you as you write the paper to make sure that you have correctly interpreted a quote you are using in support of one of your points.

Using *Shakespeare Made Easy* will pave your way to a far better understanding of and appreciation for Shakespeare's plays and will remove the textual difficulties that may have caused you to stumble in past attempts. Not only will you gain confidence in discussing the plot and characters of the play, but you will also develop a greater awareness of the ways in which Shakespeare used language for poetic expression as well as for raising intriguing and challenging moral and philosophical issues.

Ever since the works of William Shakespeare entered the canon of English literature, they have aroused the admiration of generations of scholars, readers, and theatergoers. Even if you've had negative experiences in the past with Shakespeare's plays—in fact, especially if you've had negative experiences—you will find yourself pleasantly surprised at just how entertaining his plays can be. We're glad you've chosen *Shakespeare Made Easy* as a companion on your journey to a better understanding of the plays of William Shakespeare.

William Shakespeare

His Life

Considering the impact that William Shakespeare has had on English literature, surprisingly little is known about his life. We do know that he was born to a prominent wool and leather merchant and his wife in 1564 (the actual day is in doubt but tradition sets it at April 23) in Stratford-upon-Avon, England. He is believed to have been educated at the local grammar school, although no lists of pupils survive from the sixteenth century. He did not attend university.

We also know from parish records that he married Anne Hathaway in 1582 when he was eighteen and she was twenty-six. They had three children; Susanna was their eldest, followed by twins, Judith and Hamnet. Their son, Hamnet, died at the age of about eleven, but the two daughters, Susanna and Judith, reached adulthood.

There are many stories about Shakespeare's life, such as the one alleging that he fled Stratford after having been caught poaching deer in the park belonging to Sir Thomas Lucy, a local justice of the peace. Like the rest of the tales about Shakespeare during this period of his life, this story cannot be verified and is probably untrue. Because his plays demonstrate extensive knowledge about a variety of subjects, articles have been written "proving" that Shakespeare must have temporarily pursued a career in either law, botany, or medicine or spent time as a soldier or sailor, to name a few of the occupations that he is speculated to have had.

The truth is, we simply don't know for sure what Shakespeare did for a living in the ten years following his marriage to Anne Hathaway. Ordinarily, as the eldest son he would have been expected to take over his father's business, but again there is no evidence to show that he did (or, for that matter, did not) serve an apprenticeship to his father. He may have spent some time with a traveling troupe of actors, but, aside from the baptismal records for his children, we have no actual records about him from the time of his marriage to Hathaway until 1592, by which time he had left Stratford and traveled to London. His wife and children remained in Stratford.

The next documented evidence pertaining to Shakespeare comes in 1592, when Shakespeare received his first critical recognition. It came in the form of a petulant outburst by fellow playwright Robert Greene who, apparently annoyed by the attention being received by this newcomer, complained bitterly in a pamphlet written from his deathbed about the "upstart crow . . . Shake-scene."

From about 1594 onward, Shakespeare was associated with a new theatrical company, The Lord Chamberlain's Men; by 1599 Shakespeare had become a shareholder in the company. The troupe gave command performances for Queen Elizabeth I as well as her successor, King James I. After King James' accession to the throne, the troupe took the name "The King's Men."

The King's Men performed at *The Globe* theater, which they owned. Of course, *The Globe* was not the only theater in London. *The Curtain* (built in 1577) and *The Rose* (1587), as well as a number of other theaters, also provided entertainment to the citizens. In addition to these open-air "public" theaters, there were many "private" or indoor theaters. Shakespeare and his friends purchased one of the private theaters, *The Blackfriars*, which was giving them especially stiff competition because of the popularity of the child actors who performed there.

With so many theaters in operation, the demand for plays was high. Shakespeare may have earned a living for a time by reworking older plays and by collaborating with others on new ones, and of course he also wrote his own plays. In addition to the uncertainty about many facts pertaining to his life, there even is debate about the exact number of plays Shakespeare wrote; some say he wrote thirty-seven, others say thirty-eight.

Shakespeare stopped writing for the stage in about 1611, and, having prospered not only from his writing but also from his shares in the theatrical company, he retired to Stratford, where he installed his family in New Place, one of the more expensive homes in Stratford. He died at the age of fifty-two on April 23, 1616.

His Plays

Many people are surprised to learn that none of the original handwritten manuscripts of Shakespeare's plays survives. At that time, plays were not considered to be "literature" in the same way that poetry was. In fact, when Shakespeare wrote his plays, they would have been the property of the producing company, which was concerned, not with publication of the plays, but with producing them on stage. The company would have bought them for about ten pounds apiece, and when a play finished its theatrical run and the copies were of no further use to the company, they often were discarded.

Roughly half of Shakespeare's plays were published during his lifetime in quarto (17 centimeters by 21 centimeters) volumes, although many of these were pirated copies. Booksellers often would hire someone to take shorthand notes during a performance, and then they would sell these unauthorized copies. This method for acquiring a copy of the play, needless to say, could result in numerous errors depending on the accuracy of the transcriber. In other instances of piracy, actors' scripts were purchased by a bookseller after the play had completed its run, but since each actor's copy would contain only his scenes, the actor would have to provide the rest of the text from memory, which often proved faulty. These pirated copies are referred to as "bad" Quartos. Even when a printer was working from a good manuscript (probably a prompt copy obtained from the theater), mistakes often contaminated the printed copy. In addition to all these problems, portions of the plays were sometimes censored for a variety of reasons, resulting in still further corruption of the text.

Fortunately, seven years after Shakespeare's death an authoritative version of his works, the First Folio (21 centimeters by 34 centimeters), edited by two of his theatrical partners and fellow actors, John Hemming and Henry Condell, was published. They claimed in the introduction to have used his original manuscripts, but that claim is unverified. The First Folio contained thirty-six of his plays and was titled *Comedies, Histories, and Tragedies*. Despite the Folio's apparent superiority to other printings of Shakespeare's plays, serious questions remain, and debate continues concerning discrepancies between the various early editions.

Because of the discrepancies between different editions of the plays, when one of Shakespeare's plays is published, editors must make decisions about which version to use. Often, the edition will contain lines from several of the oldest texts, but since in some cases there remains significant disagreement about which text is the "best" or most accurate, the reader may discover that there are differences between editions of the play. Many editions include notes at the end of the play to indicate the words or lines that have an alternate reading.

His Theater

In Elizabethan times, the London authorities viewed playgoing as both morally and politically questionable; they also believed that the large crowds that attended the plays created an increased risk for spreading the bubonic plague. In fact, the playhouses were closed twice during Shakespeare's lifetime as a result of outbreaks of the plague. Because of the hostile atmosphere created by the civil authorities, playhouses were typically built outside the city limits in order to place them beyond the jurisdiction of authorities.

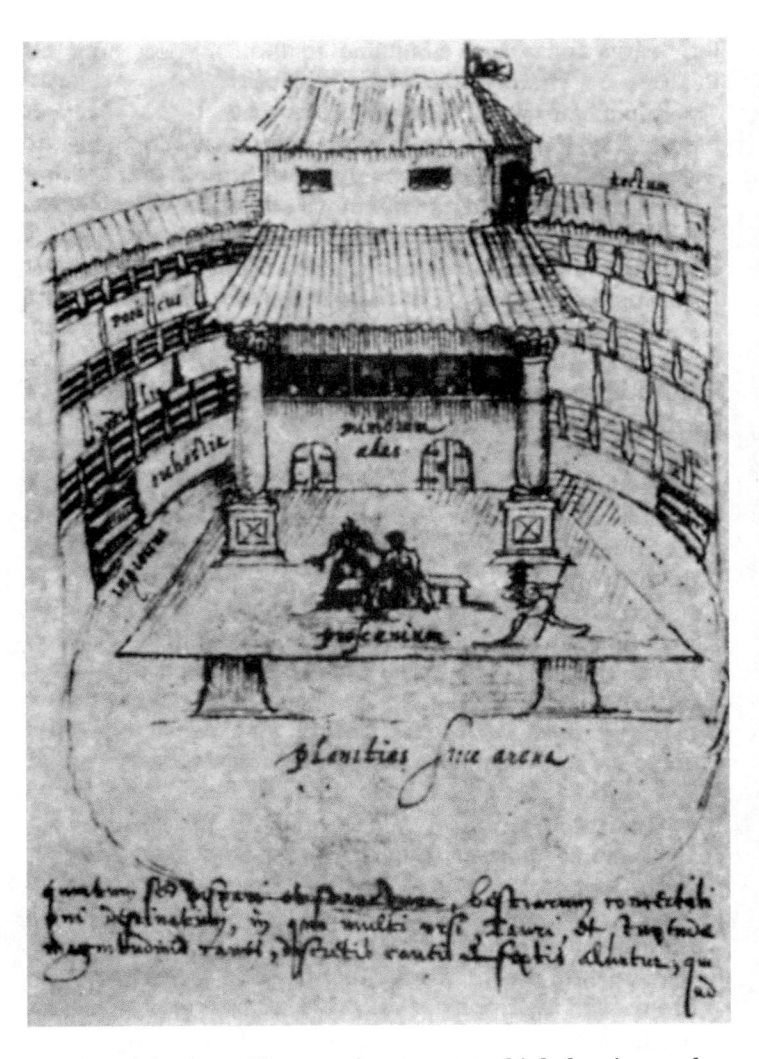

Interior of the Swan Theatre—from a pen and ink drawing made in 1596 (Mansell Collection)

When The Lord Chamberlain's Men (the troupe to which Shakespeare belonged), first began performing, *The Theater*, owned by Richard and Cuthbert Burbage, was their theatrical home. Constructed in 1576 just outside the city limits of London, *The Theater* was the first of the public playhouses. Plays had previously been performed in England in the square- or rectangular-shaped yards of the inns where traveling bands of actors stayed, but this arrangement had a serious drawback—it was far too easy for customers to enter and leave the grounds without paying the price of admission. Playhouses like *The Theater* were therefore a significant improvement since the enclosed design made it possible to have a single opening where tickets could be taken from those entering.

The Chamberlain's Men were financially successful, but a problem arose in 1598 concerning the property on which *The Theater* stood. The owner of the property planned to have the playhouse torn down once the lease on the land expired, so in late 1598 The Chamberlain's Men dismantled the building and reassembled it a short distance from the south bank of the River Thames, renaming it *The Globe*.

In 1603, The Lord Chamberlain's Men regrouped under the patronage of King James I and took the name The King's Men; the shareholders were thenceforward considered to be members of the royal household. Unfortunately, the company's fortunes took a downturn in 1613 when, during a performance of *Henry VIII*, a cannon was fired, setting the thatched roof of *The Globe* ablaze. Within an hour, the building was destroyed.

The King's Men rebuilt the playhouse, and the new *The Globe* theater, completed in 1614, was circular in shape. The "wooden O" (as it is referred to in *Henry V*) of *The Globe* actually had twenty sides, with an outer diameter of about one hundred yards. Some historians have estimated that it could hold up to three thousand people, but others dispute that figure as being far too high.

Playbills would be posted around the city to advertise for new plays, but due to the fact that the roofs of "public" theaters such as *The Globe* were open to the elements, plays could be performed only in daylight and in good weather. The theatrical company would fly a flag from the roof of the building to notify people if a performance was to proceed. If, however, the flag was not flown, theatergoers would be spared an unnecessary trip.

Those attending a play paid the gatekeeper at the entrance. In addition to standing room around the stage, seats were available in the three tiers of the gallery which encircled the playhouse. For the price of one penny (about sixty cents today), the "groundlings," as they were called, gained admission to the pit. Those who could afford to do so paid for gallery seating; the lowest tier was the least expensive, with the price climbing to as high as one shilling (about seven dollars today) for seats in the uppermost tier. The roof shielded the patrons seated in the galleries either from the heat of the sun or, in case the weather turned bad, from a sudden downpour.

Plays typically had a theatrical run of ten performances, although, depending on the popularity of the piece, some were performed up to about sixteen times; less popular plays, however, might have only six performances. The performances proceeded without intermission and usually took about two hours, although a number of Shakespeare's plays run significantly longer. When the play was about to begin, a trumpet would sound three times.

Shakespeare's plays were performed on what is referred to as a "thrust" stage; it was about five feet high and measured $27\frac{1}{2}$ feet deep by 43 feet wide; it probably sloped downward at the front (downstage) and projected out into the pit. The stage was covered by a roof (referred to as "the heavens"), which was painted to resemble a starlit sky upon which the signs of the zodiac were depicted. The area beneath the stage was referred to as "hell"; a trapdoor in the floor of the stage allowed for the entrances and exits of ghosts, monsters, and devils.

There was no scenery, nor was there a curtain that could be closed at the end of scenes or acts, so playwrights used the lines spoken by the actors to set the scene and to indicate when a scene or act was ending. A rhyming couplet, for example, would often indicate the conclusion of a scene. The gallery directly behind the stage was used for scenes in which actors were required to be either in an upper story of a house, on the battlements of a castle, or in some other elevated position. Musicians and even spectators also occupied the gallery.

At the rear of the stage (upstage) was the "tiring house" where the actors dressed (attired themselves). The tiring house had two or three doors providing access to the stage. Even though many of the plays performed were set in earlier times, the actors did not wear period costumes; the period in which a play was set would merely be suggested by certain period touches in the costumes, such as spears or helmets. Consequently, a play such as *Julius Caesar* which was set around 44 B.C.E. would have been performed in the current fashions of Elizabethan England. However, despite being historically inaccurate, the costumes the actors wore were quite lavish and were therefore not a disappointment to the audience.

Since it was illegal for women to perform in public at that time, boys or young men played the women's roles in the plays. Often, in order for a boy actor to be tall enough to be convincing in the role of an adult woman, he had to wear chopines (wooden platforms strapped to the soles of the shoes); the long skirts, which were fashionable, hid the chopines from view. Because of the restriction on women performing, Shakespeare's plays had few female characters, and, in many of his plays, the heroine would spend much of the play disguised as a boy.

The plays of Shakespeare were of course crucial to the success of the company, but the troupe also had the most renowned actor of the time, Richard Burbage. Burbage was the first actor to portray Hamlet. Although Shakespeare was himself an actor, he is only known to have performed secondary roles.

Other noted actors in the troupe were William Kempe, a comedian, and Robert Asmin, a singer and dancer, both of whom were also shareholders in The King's Men. The average size for a theatrical company was twenty-five members, about half of whom would usually be shareholders. Other actors were employed part-time as needed.

Because actors in Shakespeare's time needed to project their voices for open-air performances, they tended to employ a more exaggerated, declamatory style of acting than would be acceptable to today's audiences. Some actors went to extremes, however. Shakespearean scholars generally agree that Hamlet's instruction to the Players not to "tear a passion . . . to very rags" reflects his views on the tendency to overact amongst his contemporaries. Shakespeare's presence during rehearsals of his plays would have given him the opportunity to personally instruct an actor in the way a line should be delivered.

His Verse

Although Shakespeare's dramatic output alone would have been sufficient to ensure his place among English writers, his reputation as an author does not rest solely upon his plays. He wrote poetry, as well, including the erotic narrative poems *Venus and Adonis* (1593) and *The Rape of Lucrece* (1594). He also composed 154 *Sonnets*, which were circulated in manuscript prior to their publication in 1609.

Shakespeare's poetic output was not confined to his poems, however. At the beginning of Shakespeare's career as a playwright, the prevailing style for dialog was rhyming couplets (that is, two succeeding lines of poetry that rhyme), so a high percentage of the lines in his earlier plays rhyme. In one of his early works, *Love's Labor's Lost*, for example, nearly half of the lines rhyme.

As time passed, however, Shakespeare used fewer rhymed couplets for dialog and began favoring blank verse for his plays. Blank verse consists of unrhymed lines of iambic pentameter; iambic pentameter is the technical term for lines ten syllables in length with alternating stresses (that is, an unstressed syllable followed by a stressed syllable). Although Shakespeare continued to use rhyming couplets in his plays when he wanted to indicate the end of a scene or when the situation might call for a more artificial style of speech, he favored a much more naturalistic form of expression in his later plays.

Even in his early plays, however, Shakespeare was outdoing his fellow playwrights. For example, because of the prevailing style of rhyming couplets, most of the characters in a play would sound the same; in other words, one character's "voice" could not be distinguished from that of another. In contrast, even early on Shakespeare's characters each spoke with a recognizable voice. Even without the speaker's identity being revealed, no one would have any difficulty distinguishing the innocent yet passionate utterances of Juliet from the prosaic vulgarity of her Nurse. Furthermore, if, during the course of a play, a character underwent a significant change, Shakespeare would indicate this change by altering the character's speech patterns. One example of this technique is Othello who begins to sound more and more like Iago as he becomes progressively more infected with the "pestilence" Iago pours into his ear.

Shakespeare also used speech patterns to indicate a character's social rank. In his plays, members of the nobility usually speak in blank verse, while those of lower station speak in prose, reflecting their limited education. Shakespeare also uses prose to indicate when the more highly ranked characters are speaking informally or are under stress.

Another one of the many noteworthy aspects of Shakespeare's technique is his use of setting to reinforce ideas in his plays. In *Antony and Cleopatra*, for example, the cold austerity of Rome reflects the emotional coldness and sterility of the Romans, whereas the sun-drenched setting of Egypt reflects the passionate love of the title characters.

Furthermore, Shakespeare used imagery not only to create atmosphere but also to convey themes. *Hamlet*, for example, contains numerous references to disease and decay, reinforcing the theme of the moral and political rot in Denmark. In addition to demonstrating his technical brilliance, Shakespeare's works reveal insights into human nature that none of his predecessors or contemporaries could begin to approach.

Shakespeare's technique and contributions to drama and literature place him at the pinnacle of his art. It's no surprise then that each succeeding generation sees new additions to the ranks of "Bardolators."

Much Ado About Nothing

Date

It is believed that *Much Ado About Nothing* was written in mid-to late 1598 primarily because of the character Dogberry. This character was written specifically for an actor named Will Kempe, a leading Elizabethan comedian. Kempe left Shakespeare's theatre company, The Lord Chamberlain's Men, in January or February of 1599. Kempe's name appears accidentally in the 1600 quarto edition. The play itself was officially registered with the Stationer's Company on August 2, 1600. As mentioned above, the play was first published in the Andrew Wise and William Aspley quarto edition dated 1600. The next known publication of *Much Ado About Nothing* was in the First Folio of 1623. It is not known whether or not the play was performed before May 1613, when it was staged twice for Princess Elizabeth's engagement and marriage. At the time of the staging, it was titled *Benedicke and Betteris*.

Source

The plot of *Much Ado About Nothing* is an example of the traditional European story of a lover who is tricked into believing that his beloved has been unfaithful. Stories such as these date back to late classical times. Shakespeare drew inspiration for this play from an epic poem titled *Orlando Furioso* written by Ludovico Ariosto. The Italian edition was published in 1532 and the English translation by Sir John Harrington in 1591, and Shakespeare might have used both versions. It is believed that Shakespeare also used an adaptation of Ariosto's poem written by Matteo Bandello and published in 1554. Most of the details of the courtship between Claudio and Hero are foreshadowed in these two texts; however, Claudio's rejection of Hero at their wedding is suggested in an English version of Ariosto's story by George Whetstone that appears in his book titled *The Rock of Regard*, a collection of stories published in 1576.

Although the Ariosto and Bandello texts contributed to Shakespeare's inspiration for the Claudio and Hero characters, the Dogberry character is strictly his own invention. The confused speech and nonsensical logic of this character, however, had been a theatrical staple for quite awhile. In fact, Shakespeare had incorporated a similar character in *Love's Labour's Lost* with the minor character Constable Dull. The Beatrice and Benedick characters also come from a well-established tradition of the sixteenth century. One of the most widely read books of the time, *The Book of the Courtier*, published in 1528 and written by the Italian Baldassare Castiglione, certainly inspired Shakespeare's most beloved characters, Beatrice and Benedick. Although much of the characters' verbal sparring is Shakespeare's own invention, Castiglione presents the idea that women have much to contribute to an ideal courtly life, and he illustrates this point with a series of energetic debates between a man and a woman.

Text

The 1600 quarto edition was typeset from what are known as Shakespeare's "foul papers." These foul papers were written by Shakespeare and were quite messy, hence their name. He often used the names of the actors for whom he was writing the parts instead of the characters' names. For instance, Kempe's name is used for Dogberry and Richard Cowley for Verges. Additionally, the foul papers were rather like rough drafts because entrances and exits are omitted and speech prefixes are inconsistent. A ghost character is mentioned in these papers as well. Innogen, who is Leonato's wife and Hero's mother, is mentioned in the opening stage directions of the quarto but never appears after that. The Folio text is derived from a copy of the quarto but it is supplemented with stage directions that have been either added in or elaborated upon.

This play has been one of the most popular of Shakespeare's comedies since about the mid-eighteenth century. The Benedick and Beatrice characters have inspired many other works on their own merit. Hector Berlioz wrote an operatic version of the two characters titled *Béatrice et Bénédict* in 1861. William Davenant borrowed the couple in his 1662 development of a Restoration play titled *The Law Against Lovers*.

Much Ado About Nothing has traversed the stage and screen regularly for hundreds of years since its initial introduction in the early1600s. By intertwining the serious love affair between Claudio and Hero with their comedic opposites in Beatrice and Benedick, and by adding a touch of Dogberry, Shakespeare has and will continue to capture attention with this play for many years to come.

Much Ado About Nothing

Original Text and Modern Version

The Characters

Leonato	Governor of Messina
Hero	daughter of Leonato
Beatrice	niece of Leonato
Antonio	Leonato's brother
Ursula	servant to Hero
Margaret	servant to Hero
Don Pedro	Prince of Aragon
Count Claudio	a nobleman from Florence
Benedick	a gentleman from Padua
Balthasar	musician and singer employed by Don Pedro
Don John	half brother of Don Pedro
Conrade	follower of Don John
Borachio	follower of Don John
Dogberry	policeman of Messina
Verges	partner and second in command to Dogberry
George Seacoal	leader of the watchmen
First Watchman	
Second Watchman	
Sexton	documents Dogberry's interrogation
Friar Francis	clergyman
Messenger to Leonato	
Messenger to Don Pedro	
Boy, Musicians, Lords, Attendants	

Synopsis

Act I

Scene I   At Leonato's house in Messina
Don Pedro's army arrives in Messina after a battle.

Scene II   A room in Leonato's house
Leonato believes erroneously that Don Pedro wishes to marry his daughter.

Scene III   Another room in Leonato's home
Don John wants to obstruct the marriage between Claudio and Hero.

Act II

Scene I   In the house of Leonato
Hero and Claudio become engaged, and a plan to trick Beatrice and Benedick into falling in love is devised.

Scene II   A room in Leonato's house
Don John and Borachio plan to disrupt the marriage.

Scene III   In the gardens of Leonato's home
Benedick overhears a staged conversation about Beatrice's love for him.

Act III

Scene I   Under the arbors of Leonato's garden
Beatrice overhears a staged conversation about Benedick's love for her.

Scene II   A room in Leonato's home
Don John tells Don Pedro and Claudio of Hero's alleged unfaithfulness.

Scene III   In and around the city of Messina
The night watchmen discover Borachio and Don Pedro's trickery.

Act one

Scene 1

Enter **Leonato**, *governor of Messina*, **Hero** *his daughter, and* **Beatrice** *his niece, with a* **Messenger**.

Leonato I learn in this letter that Don [Pedro] of Arragon comes this night to Messina.

Messenger He is very near by this, he was not three leagues off when I left him.

Leonato How many gentlemen have you lost in this
6 action?

Messenger But few of any sort, and none of name.

Leonato A victory is twice itself when the achiever brings home full numbers. I find here that Don [Pedro] hath bestow'd much honor on a young
11 Florentine call'd Claudio.

Messenger Much deserv'd on his part, and equally rememb'red by Don Pedro. He hath borne himself beyond the promise of his age, doing in the figure of a lamb the feats of a lion. He hath indeed better bett'red expectation than you must expect of me
17 to tell you how.

Leonato He hath an uncle here in Messina will be very much glad of it.

Messenger I have already deliver'd him letters, and there appears much joy in him, even so much that joy could not show itself modest enough without a badge of bitterness.

Act one

Scene 1

Standing in front of his home, **Leonato**, *with his daughter* **Hero** *and niece* **Beatrice**, *receives a letter delivered by a messenger of* **Don Pedro** *of Aragon.*

Leonato   The letter states that Don Pedro of Aragon will be arriving in Messina this evening.

Messenger   Yes, he is very close; when I left he was only about nine miles away.

Leonato   How many gentlemen were killed in this most recent battle?

Messenger   Very few were lost and none of any importance or ranking.

Leonato   A battle victory is twice as rewarding when few men are lost in the process. The letter also states that Don Pedro is honoring a young man from Florence named Claudio.

Messenger   The honor given to him by Don Pedro is well deserved. In battle, Claudio performed far beyond his years and level of experience. Although he appears to be a lamb, his actions proved equal to those of a lion. I cannot do justice in telling all that he has accomplished.

Leonato   His uncle here in Messina will be extremely happy to hear of his accomplishments and honors.

Messenger   I have delivered the letters to him already and he seems very happy. In fact he seemed so happy that his facial expression seemed grief-stricken.

Leonato   Did he break out into tears?

25 **Messenger**   In great measure.

Leonato   A kind overflow of kindness. There are
no faces truer than those that are so wash'd. How
much better is it to weep at joy than to joy at weeping!

Beatrice   I pray you, is Signior Mountanto return'd
31 from the wars or no?

Messenger   I know none of that name, lady. There
was none such in the army of any sort.

Leonato   What is he that you ask for, niece?

Hero   My cousin means Signior Benedick of
36 Padua.

Messenger   O, he's return'd, and as pleasant as ever
he was.

Beatrice   He set up his bills here in Messina, and
40 challeng'd Cupid at the flight, and my uncle's
fool, reading the challenge, subscrib'd for Cupid,
and challeng'd him at the burbolt. I pray you, how
many hath he kill'd and eaten in these wars? But
how many hath he kill'd? for indeed I promis'd to eat
45 all of his killing.

Leonato   Faith, niece, you tax Signior Benedick too
much, but he'll be meet with you, I doubt it not.

Messenger   He hath done good service, lady, in these
49 wars.

Beatrice   You had musty victual, and he hath holp
to eat it. He is a very valiant trencherman; he hath
an excellent stomach.

Leonato   Did he begin to cry?

Messenger   He was sobbing.

Leonato   That in itself is a true sign of kindness and affection. It is far better to cry for happiness than to find happiness in crying.

Beatrice   Please tell me, has Signior Mountanto [*the great fencer and bully*] returned from the wars or not?

Messenger   I don't know anyone by that name, miss; there wasn't anyone in the army that fits that description.

Leonato   Who are you asking about, niece?

Hero   My cousin is wondering about Signior Benedick of Padua.

Messenger   Oh, he has returned and is as jovial and happy as always.

Beatrice   He posted flyers around Messina challenging Cupid [*the god of love*] to an archery contest. When my uncle's clown read the challenge, he responded using Cupid's name and challenged Signior Benedick to a bird hunt with toy arrows. Please tell me, how many men has Benedick killed and eaten in these battles? Well, at least tell me how many he has killed because I promised to eat all of his killing.

Leonato   Honestly, niece, you criticize Signior Benedick far too much, but I have no doubt whatsoever that he will get even with your mockery.

Messenger   Miss, he has provided fine service in these battles.

Beatrice   You had stale food and he certainly helped eat it. He has a healthy appetite and a brave and courageous stomach.

Messenger   And a good soldier too, lady.

Beatrice   And a good soldier to a lady, but what is
55   he to a lord?

Messenger   A lord to a lord, a man to a man, stuff'd
with all honorable virtues.

Beatrice   It is so indeed, he is no less than a stuff'd
man. But for the stuffing—well, we are all mor-
60   tal.

Leonato   You must not, sir, mistake my niece. There
is a kind of merry war betwixt Signior Benedick
and her; they never meet but there's a skirmish of wit
64   between them.

Beatrice   Alas, he gets nothing by that. In our last
conflict four of his five wits went halting off, and
now is the whole man govern'd with one; so that
if he have wit enough to keep himself warm, let
him bear it for a difference between himself and
70   his horse, for it is all the wealth that he hath left
to be known a reasonable creature. Who is his
companion now? he hath every month a new sworn
brother.

74 **Messenger**   Is't possible?

Beatrice   Very easily possible. He wears his faith
but as the fashion of his hat: it ever changes with
the next block.

Messenger   I see, lady, the gentleman is not in your
79   books.

Beatrice   No, and he were, I would burn my study.
But I pray you, who is his companion? Is there no
young squarer now that will make a voyage with
him to the devil?

Messenger   He is a good soldier as well, miss.

Beatrice   He may be a good soldier in comparison to a lady, but how does he compare to a lord?

Messenger   Truthfully, he is a lord to a lord and a man to a man; he is filled with respectable qualities.

Beatrice   Certainly that is true, he is stuffed much like a mannequin, but as for what he is stuffed with, well, we are human after all.

Leonato   Please, sir, do not misunderstand my niece. There is a cheerful battle of wits between her and Signior Benedick every time the two of them meet.

Beatrice   Oh my! He seriously cannot win. In our last conflict, four of his five wits deserted him, leaving him with only one. So if he has enough intelligence to keep himself warm, allow him to hold on to it because that would be the only difference between he and his horse and therefore all the wealth that he has left in the world. But who is he hanging around with these days? He usually has a new best friend every month.

Messenger   Is that possible?

Beatrice   It is extremely possible. He changes his friendship and loyalties just as he changes the style of his hat, according to whatever fashion is popular at the time.

Messenger   I see, miss, that the gentleman is obviously not one of your chosen books [*favorite people*].

Beatrice   No, he isn't. And, if he were I would burn my library. But please, tell me, who is his friend right now? Isn't there any young hooligan that would escort him to visit with the devil?

Messenger   He is most in the company of the right
85   noble Claudio.

Beatrice   O Lord, he will hang upon him like a disease; he is sooner caught than the pestilence, and
the taker runs presently mad. God help the noble
Claudio! If he have caught the Benedick, it will
90   cost him a thousand pound ere 'a be cur'd.

Messenger   I will hold friends with you, lady.

Beatrice   Do, good friend.

Leonato   You will never run mad, niece.

Beatrice   No, not till a hot January.

95   **Messenger**   Don Pedro is approach'd.

Enter **Don Pedro**, **Claudio**, **Benedick**, **Balthasar**, *and*
[Don] John *the Bastard.*

Don Pedro   Good Signior Leonato, are you come
to meet your trouble? The fashion of the world is to
avoid cost, and you encounter it.

Leonato   Never came trouble to my house in the
100   likeness of your Grace, for trouble being gone,
comfort should remain; but when you depart from
me, sorrow abides and happiness takes his leave.

Don Pedro   You embrace your charge too willingly.
104   I think this is your daughter.

Leonato   Her mother hath many times told me so.

Benedick   Were you in doubt, sir, that you ask'd her?

Messenger   At the present, he and Claudio are good friends.

Beatrice   Goodness. He will hover around him like a disease and once this disease has caught the victim, he will run mad. God help Claudio if he should catch the Benedick disease; it will surely cost him a thousand pounds before he is cured.

Messenger   I surely want to remain your friend, miss.

Beatrice   Do exactly that, my good friend.

Leonato   You are never going to fall victim to this Benedick disease, niece.

Beatrice   No, not until there is a hot January.

Messenger   Don Pedro is approaching.

[**Don Pedro, Don John, Claudio, Benedick,** and **Balthasar** join **Leonato, Hero, Beatrice,** and the **Messenger.**]

Don Pedro   Dear Signior Leonato, do you know what kind of trouble you are in by welcoming me and my army? Most of the world tends to avoid such an expensive burden, but you seem to welcome it.

Leonato   You could never be a burden in my house. But when trouble leaves, an easier life remains. However, when you leave, sadness takes over and happiness is nowhere to be found.

Don Pedro   Sir, I think you are far too willing to take on this enormous challenge. [*turning to Hero*] This must be your daughter.

Leonato   Yes, her mother assured me that was true.

Benedick   You must have had cause to doubt, is that why you asked her?

108 **Leonato**   Signior Benedick, no, for then were you a child.

Don Pedro   You have it full, Benedick. We may
guess by this what you are, being a man. Truly,
the lady fathers herself. Be happy, lady, for you are
112 like an honorable father.

Benedick   If Signior Leonato be her father, she would
not have his head on her shoulders for all Messina,
115 as like him as she is.

Beatrice   I wonder that you will still be talking,
Signior Benedick, nobody marks you.

Benedick   What, my dear Lady Disdain! are you yet
119 living?

Beatrice   Is it possible disdain should die while she
hath such meet food to feed it as Signior Benedick?
Courtesy itself must convert to disdain, if you come
in her presence.

Benedick   Then is courtesy a turncoat. But it is
125 certain I am lov'd of all ladies, only you excepted;
and I would I could find in my heart that I had not a
hard heart, for truly I love none.

Beatrice   A dear happiness to women, they would
else have been troubled with a pernicious suitor.
130 I thank God and my cold blood, I am of your
humor for that: I had rather hear my dog bark at a
crow than a man swear he loves me.

Benedick   God keep your ladyship still in that mind!
so some gentleman or other shall scape a predes-
135 tinate scratch'd face.

Beatrice   Scratching could not make it worse, and
'twere such a face as yours were.

Leonato   No, Signior Benedick, because at that time you were yet a child and I would have had no cause to doubt her.

Don Pedro   You got what you deserved with that answer Benedick; he surely knows your reputation with women. Honestly, it is obvious who her father is, she resembles Leonato so strongly. Miss, you should be pleased that you look like such an honorable man.

Benedick   Despite the strong resemblance to Signior Leonato, I doubt that she would want to have his head on her body for all of Messina.

Beatrice   Why are you still speaking, Signior Benedick? No one is paying any attention to you.

Benedick   Surprise! It is my dear Lady Disdain. You haven't died yet?

Beatrice   It would be impossible for disdain to die with such suitable food to feed upon as Signior Benedick; even courtesy changes into disdain every time you make your presence known.

Benedick   So, courtesy is a traitor. I am definitely loved by all women, all except you that is. And I wish that I didn't have such a hard heart, because I sincerely love no one.

Beatrice   That truly means happiness to women; otherwise they would be troubled by a wicked suitor. I thank God and my cold blood that I am like you in that respect. I'd rather hear my dog bark at a crow than to hear a man swear his love for me.

Benedick   May God keep you thinking that way so that some man will not inevitably end up with a scratched face.

Beatrice   A scratching would not make it worse, especially if it were a face like yours.

Benedick   Well, you are a rare parrot-teacher.

Beatrice   A bird of my tongue is better than a beast
140   of yours.

Benedick   I would my horse had the speed of your
tongue, and so good a continuer. But keep your way,
a' God's name, I have done.

Beatrice   You always end with a jade's trick, I know
145   you of old.

Don Pedro   That is the sum of all: Leonato—
Signior Claudio and Signior Benedick—my dear
friend Leonato hath invited you all. I tell him we
shall stay here at the least a month, and he heartily
150   prays some occasion may detain us longer. I
dare swear he is no hypocrite, but prays from his
heart.

Leonato   If you swear, my lord, you shall not be
forsworn. [*To Don John*] Let me bid you welcome,
my lord, being reconcil'd to the Prince your brother:
156   I owe you all duty.

Don John   I thank you. I am not of many words,
but I thank you.

159 **Leonato**   Please it your Grace lead on?

Don Pedro   Your hand, Leonato, we will go together.

Exeunt. Manent Benedick and Claudio.

Benedick   Well, you continue to repeat yourself as if you are teaching a parrot to speak.

Beatrice   A bird who speaks with a tongue like mine is better than a beast who cannot speak with a tongue like yours.

Benedick   I wish my horse had the speed of your tongue and the endurance. But have it your way, in God's name; I am finished.

Beatrice   You always drop out of a match like an ill-conditioned horse who cannot finish a race: I remember you from past experiences.

Don Pedro   Well, it is decided then, Leonato. Signior Claudio and Signior Benedick, my dear friend Leonato has invited you all to stay. And when I told him that we would be staying for at least a month, he hoped that something might detain us longer. I know that he is not a fraud but truly speaks from his heart.

Leonato   If you promise, my lord, you will not be called a liar.

[*Leonato turns to Don John.*] Allow me to welcome you, Don John. After having rekindled my friendship with your brother the Prince, I owe you the same welcome.

Don John   Thank you: I am not a man of many words, but thank you nonetheless.

Leonato   Please, your honor, will you lead the way?

Don Pedro   Give me your hand, Leonato; we will go together.

[*Everyone leaves except Benedick and Claudio.*]

Claudio   Benedick, didst thou note the daughter of
Signior Leonato?

Benedick   I noted her not, but I look'd on her.

165 **Claudio**   Is she not a modest young lady?

Benedick   Do you question me, as an honest man
should do, for my simple true judgment? or would
you have me speak after my custom, as being a
169   profess'd tyrant to their sex?

Claudio   No, I pray thee speak in sober judgment.

Benedick   Why, i' faith, methinks she's too low for a
high praise, too brown for a fair praise, and too little
for a great praise; only this commendation I can
afford her, that were she other than she is, she were
unhandsome, and being no other but as she is, I do
176   not like her.

Claudio   Thou thinkest I am in sport. I pray thee
tell me truly how thou lik'st her.

Benedick   Would you buy her, that you inquire after
180   her?

Claudio   Can the world buy such a jewel?

Benedick   Yea, and a case to put it into. But speak
you this with a sad brow? or do you play the flouting
Jack, to tell us Cupid is a good hare-finder and
Vulcan a rare carpenter? Come, in what key shall a
186   man take you to go in the song?

Claudio   In mine eye, she is the sweetest lady that
ever I look'd on.

Claudio   Benedick, did you notice Signior Leonato's daughter?

Benedick   I looked at her, but I didn't really notice her.

Claudio   Don't you think she is a well-bred young woman?

Benedick   Are you asking for the simple truth as you would ask any man, or are you asking an opinion from someone who cruelly insults those of the female sex?

Claudio   No, please, speak seriously.

Benedick   Well, truthfully, I think she's too short for high praise, too dark for fair praise, and too small for great praise. The only thing I can say positively about her is that if she were anything else, she would be ugly, but considering her as she is, I do not like her.

Claudio   Do you think I am joking? Please, tell me the truth, how do you like her?

Benedick   Why are you asking? Are you thinking of buying her?

Claudio   Would anyone be able to buy such a beautiful gem?

Benedick   Of course you can buy such a gem, and a case to put it in as well. Are you serious about this or are you mockingly telling us that Cupid, who is blind, can find rabbits and that Vulcan, the blacksmith of the gods, is a great carpenter? Let me know what key you are singing in so that I can join in with you.

Claudio   To me she is the sweetest woman that I have ever seen.

Benedick   I can see yet without spectacles, and I see
190   no such matter. There's her cousin, and she
were not possess'd with a fury, exceeds her as much in
beauty as the first of May doth the last of December.
But I hope you have no intent to turn husband,
194   have you?

   Claudio   I would scarce trust myself, though I had
sworn the contrary, if Hero would be my wife.

Benedick   Is't come to this? In faith, hath not the
world one man but he will wear his cap with suspicion? Shall I never see a bachelor of threescore
200   again? Go to, i' faith, and thou wilt needs thrust
thy neck into a yoke, wear the print of it, and sigh
away Sundays. Look, Don Pedro is return'd to
seek you.

   Enter **Don Pedro**.

Don Pedro   What secret hath held you here, that
205   you follow'd not to Leonato's?

   Benedick   I would your grace would constrain me to
tell.

   Don Pedro   I charge thee on thy allegiance.

Benedick   You hear, Count Claudio, I can be secret
210   as a dumb man; I would have you think so; but
on my allegiance, mark you this, on my allegiance,
he is in love. With who? Now that is your Grace's
part. Mark how short his answer is: with Hero,
Leonato's short daughter.

215 **Claudio**   If this were so, so were it utt'red.

   Benedick   Like the old tale, my lord: "It is not so,
nor 'twas not so, but indeed, God forbid it should
be so."

Benedick   I can still see without glasses and I certainly don't see her in the same way. But her cousin, on the other hand, if she had less of a vile temperament, would exceed Hero in beauty like May does over December. I hope that you are not considering the idea of becoming a husband?

Claudio   Although I have sworn otherwise, I could hardly keep my vow to remain a bachelor if Hero would consent to be my wife.

Benedick   What's the world coming to? Truly, is there no man in the world who is suspicious of all women and marriage? Will I ever see a bachelor who is sixty years old again? Go ahead and lock yourself into marriage like an ox into its yoke. Disregard your freedom and spend your Sundays with your wife. Look, there's Don Pedro looking for you.

[**Don Pedro** *re-enters.*]

Don Pedro   What secrets have caused you two to stay back and not go to Leonato's with us?

Benedick   You will have to force me to tell, sir.

Don Pedro   I am asking on your honor and loyalty to confess.

Benedick   Listen, Claudio, I am able to keep a secret like a mute, but because I owe Don Pedro my loyalty, I have to tell. He is in love. And with whom you might ask? Notice how short the answer is: with Hero, Leonato's short daughter.

Claudio   If this is true, it must be as you say.

Benedick   But just like the old story goes, he tries to deny that it is not true, and it was not true, but God help us if it should be true.

Claudio   If my passion change not shortly, God
220   forbid it should be otherwise.

Don Pedro   Amen, if you love her, for the lady is
very well worthy.

Claudio   You speak this to fetch me in, my lord.

Don Pedro   By my troth, I speak my thought.

225 **Claudio**   And in faith, my lord, I spoke mine.

Benedick   And by my two faiths and troths, my
lord, I spoke mine.

Claudio   That I love her, I feel.

Don Pedro   That she is worthy, I know.

Benedick   That I neither feel how she should be lov'd,
231   nor know how she should be worthy, is the
opinion that fire cannot melt out of me; I will die in it
at the stake.

Don Pedro   Thou wast ever an obstinate heretic in
235   the despite of beauty.

Claudio   And never could maintain his part but in
the force of his will.

Benedick   That a woman conceiv'd me, I thank her;
that she brought me up, I likewise give her most
240   humble thanks; but that I will have a rechate
winded in my forehead, or hang my bugle in an
invisible baldrick, all women shall pardon me. Because I will not do them the wrong to mistrust
any, I will do myself the right to trust none; and the
fine is (for the which I may go the finer), I will live
246   a bachelor.

Don Pedro   I shall see thee, ere I die, look pale with
love.

Claudio   Unless my feelings change suddenly, God help me, but I will have to admit that it is the truth.

Don Pedro   That's great if you love her, because she is well worthy of it.

Claudio   Are you saying this to trick me, my lord?

Don Pedro   I am speaking the truth.

Claudio   And, in truth, my lord, I spoke mine.

Benedick   And, by my two beliefs and truths, my lord, I have spoken mine.

Claudio   I feel that I love her.

Don Pedro   I know that she is worthy of it.

Benedick   I have no idea how she should be loved or whether or not she is worthy, and that is an opinion that not even a fire can melt out of me. I will die at the stake believing this.

Don Pedro   You are the most stubborn nonbeliever and despiser of beauty.

Claudio   And he can never be convinced otherwise.

Benedick   That a woman conceived me, I will thank her. That a woman raised me, I will most humbly give thanks for that too. But I will not be controlled by an untrustworthy woman. All women shall excuse me, but I don't do them wrong to mistrust them, and I allow myself the right to not trust any of them. Therefore, I will live the life of a bachelor and dress that much nicer because of it.

Don Pedro   I swear that before I die, I will see you pale with love.

Benedick   With anger, with sickness, or with hunger,
my lord, not with love. Prove that ever I lose more
251   blood with love than I will get again with drinking, pick out mine eyes with a ballad-maker's pen,
and hang me up at the door of a brothel-house for the
sign of blind Cupid.

Don Pedro   Well, if ever thou dost fall from this
256   faith, thou wilt prove a notable argument.

Benedick   If I do, hang me in a bottle like a cat, and
shoot at me, and he that hits me, let him be clapp'd
on the shoulder, and call'd Adam.

260 **Don Pedro**   Well, as time shall try:
"In time the savage bull doth bear the yoke."

Benedick   The savage bull may, but if ever the sensible Benedick bear it, pluck off the bull's horns,
and set them in my forehead, and let me be vildly
painted, and in such great letters as they write
266   "Here is good horse to hire," let them signify
under my sign, "Here you may see Benedick the
married man."

Claudio   If this should ever happen, thou wouldst
270   be horn-mad.

Don Pedro   Nay, if Cupid have not spent all his
quiver in Venice, thou wilt quake for this shortly.

Benedick   I look for an earthquake too then.

Don Pedro   Well, you will temporize with the
275   hours. In the mean time, good Signior Benedick,
repair to Leonato's, commend me to him, and tell
him I will not fail him at supper, for indeed he hath
made great preparation.

Benedick   No, you will see me angry, sick, and hungry, my lord, but not in love. If I ever become more pale with love than with drinking, pick out my eyes with a ballad-maker's pen and hang me up at the door of a brothel in place of the sign of blind Cupid.

Don Pedro   Well, if you ever waver from this belief, you will certainly prove it to be a worthy cause.

Benedick   If I do waver, hang me in a bottle like a cat and allow anyone to shoot at me. And, for the one who hits me, pat him on the back and call him Adam, the hero.

Don Pedro   Well, as they say, time will tell, and the most stubborn and savage bull will wear the yoke.

Benedick   The savage bull may wear the yoke, but if the ever-sensible Benedick wears it, pull off the bull's horns and set them in my forehead. Then hang a painted sign on me as they would a horse for hire that reads, "Here you see Benedick, the married man."

Claudio   You would certainly be a raving madman if that ever happens.

Don Pedro   Certainly not. If Cupid has not used up all of his arrows in making men lovesick in Venice, he will have you trembling in a minute.

Benedick   Okay then, I'll certainly be looking for an earth-quake too.

Don Pedro   You will change as time passes, but in the meantime, good Signior Benedick, go to Leonato's and give him my respects and tell him that I will be there for supper, as I know that he has gone to great lengths in preparing for it.

Benedick   I have almost matter enough in me for
280   such an embassage, and so I commit you—

Claudio   To the tuition of God. From my house—
if I had it—

Don Pedro   The sixt of July. Your loving friend,
284   Benedick.

Benedick   Nay, mock not, mock not. The body of
your discourse is sometime guarded with fragments,
and the guards are but slightly basted on neither.
Ere you flout old ends any further, examine your
conscience, and so I leave you.

Exit.

Claudio   My liege, your Highness now may do me
290   good.

Don Pedro   My love is thine to teach; teach it but
how,
And thou shalt see how apt it is to learn
Any hard lesson that may do thee good.

Claudio   Hath Leonato any son, my lord?

Don Pedro   No child but Hero, she's his only heir.
Dost thou affect her, Claudio?

296 **Claudio**   O, my lord,
When you went onward on this ended action,
I look'd upon her with a soldier's eye,
That lik'd, but had a rougher task in hand
300   Than to drive liking to the name of love.
But now I am return'd and that war-thoughts
Have left their places vacant, in their rooms
Come thronging soft and delicate desires,
All prompting me how fair young Hero is,
305   Saying I lik'd her ere I went to wars.

Benedick I have almost enough material in me to accomplish such an assignment, and so I will make the commitment for you—

Claudio With the protection of God: From my house, if I had one,—

Don Pedro The sixth of July: Your loving friend, Benedick.

Benedick Quit fooling around. Sometimes the bits and pieces of your conversations make little if any sense, and before you continue your nonsensical banter, examine your own conscience. With that, I leave you.

[*Benedick exits.*]

Claudio My lord, you can help me here.

Don Pedro I will do anything to help you, just tell me what you want me to do. You will see how anxious I am to help, no matter how difficult the task.

Claudio Does Leonato have any sons, my lord?

Don Pedro His only child is Hero, his only heir. Do you like her, Claudio?

Claudio Oh, my lord, earlier, before we went to war, I saw her with the eyes of a soldier. A soldier who was focused on the task at hand, a war. And although I liked her, I didn't think that liking would turn to love. But, now that I am back and the thoughts of war have left my mind, in their place are soft and delicate desires telling me how beautiful young Hero is and telling me how much I liked her before I went to war.

Don Pedro   Thou wilt be like a lover presently,
And tire the hearer with a book of words.
If thou dost love fair Hero, cherish it,
And I will break with her, and with her father,
310   And thou shalt have her. Was't not to this end
That thou began'st to twist so fine a story?

Claudio   How sweetly you do minister to love,
That know love's grief by his complexion!
But lest my liking might too sudden seem,
315   I would have salv'd it with a longer treatise.

Don Pedro   What need the bridge much broader than
the flood?
The fairest grant is the necessity.
Look, what will serve is fit: 'tis once, thou lovest,
And I will fit thee with the remedy.
320   I know we shall have revelling to-night;
I will assume thy part in some disguise,
And tell fair Hero I am Claudio,
And in her bosom I'll unclasp my heart,
And take her hearing prisoner with the force
325   And strong encounter of my amorous tale;
Then after to her father will I break,
And the conclusion is, she shall be thine.
In practice let us put it presently.

Exeunt.

Don Pedro   No doubt you will be like a typical lover soon, making the listener tired with continual discussions about your thoughts of love. If you love beautiful Hero, treasure it. I will talk to her and her father and you shall have her. Wasn't this the way you wanted it to end before you began to tell such a fine story?

Claudio   You seem to know exactly what to do, and you can tell by the sight of me that I am lovesick. If my feelings appear too sudden, I could continue the story at length.

Don Pedro   There is no need for that. Why bother? That's like building a bridge that is wider than the river you are going to cross. The best gift is simply to do whatever is needed to get the job done. Tonight there is going to be a party, and I will disguise myself as you and tell beautiful Hero that I am Claudio. I will open my heart to her and make her listen to a romantic tale. Afterwards, I will speak with her father, and the end result will be that she will be yours. Let's put it into action immediately.

[*They exit.*]

Scene 2

[*Enter* **Leonato** *and an old man* [**Antonio**], *brother to Leonato,* [*meeting*].

Leonato   How now, brother, where is my cousin, your son? Hath he provided this music?

Antonio   He is very busy about it. But, brother, I can tell you strange news that you yet dreamt not
5   of.

Leonato   Are they good?

Antonio   As the [event] stamps them, but they have a good cover; they show well outward. The Prince and Count Claudio, walking in a thick-pleach'd
10   alley in mine orchard, were thus much over-heard by a man of mine. The Prince discover'd to Claudio that he lov'd my niece your daughter, and meant to acknowledge it this night in a dance; and if he found her accordant, he meant to take the present time by the top, and instantly break with
16   you of it.

Leonato   Hath the fellow any wit that told you this?

Antonio   A good sharp fellow. I will send for him,
19   and question him yourself.

Leonato   No, no, we will hold it as a dream till it appear itself; but I will acquaint my daughter withal, that she may be the better prepar'd for an answer, if peradventure this be true. Go you and tell her of it. [*Several persons cross the stage.*] Cousins, you
25   know what you have to do. O, I cry you mercy, friend, go you with me, and I will use your skill. Good cousin, have a care this busy time.

Exeunt.

Scene 2

Leonato *and his brother* **Antonio** *meet in a room inside Leonato's house.*

Leonato Hi, brother! Where is my nephew, your son? Is he preparing the music?

Antonio Yes, he is working on it. But let me tell you something, I just heard the strangest news, something you would never have thought of.

Leonato Is it good news?

Antonio It appears to be good news. A servant of mine overheard the Prince and Count Claudio while they were walking in the garden. The Prince told Claudio that he loves your daughter and will confess that love to her at the dance this evening. If she is agreeable, he intends to speak with you about it as well.

Leonato Is the servant who told you this reliable?

Antonio He is bright and honest. I will send for him if you would like to speak with him yourself.

Leonato No, no; let's pretend it is merely a dream until it actually happens. But I will inform my daughter of it so that she will be better prepared with an answer should it be true. Go and tell her about it for me.

[**Attendants** *enter.*]

Cousins, you know what needs to be done. Excuse me, please, go with me, I can use your help. Cousin, be careful during this busy time.

[*They all exit.*]

Scene 3

[*Enter* **[Don] John** *the Bastard and* **Conrade**, *his companion.*]

Conrade   What the good-year, my lord, why are
you thus out of measure sad?

Don John   There is no measure in the occasion
that breeds, therefore the sadness is without limit.

5 **Conrade**   You should hear reason.

Don John   And when I have heard it, what blessing
brings it?

Conrade   If not a present remedy, at least a patient
9   sufferance.

Don John   I wonder that thou (being, as thou say'st thou
art, born under Saturn) goest about to
apply a moral medicine to a mortifying mischief.
I cannot hide what I am: I must be sad when I
14   have cause and smile at no man's jests; eat
when I have stomach, and wait for no man's leisure;
sleep when I am drowsy, and tend on no man's business; laugh when I am merry, and claw no man in
18   his humor.

Conrade   Yea, but you must not make the full show
of this till you may do it without controlment.
You have of late stood out against your brother,
and he hath ta'en you newly into his grace, where
it is impossible you should take true root but by
the fair weather that you make yourself. It is need-
ful that you frame the season for your own har-
26   vest.

Scene 3

Enter **Don John** *and* **Conrade** *in a room inside Leonato's house.*

Conrade   Of all the diseases, my lord, why are you so sad?

Don John   There is no limit to the causes; therefore the sadness is without end.

Conrade   You should listen to reason.

Don John   And after I've listened to it, what good will come of it?

Conrade   Well, if it won't cure the problem, it will at least allow you to endure it with patience.

Don John   This is rather strange coming from someone who claims to be born under the planet Saturn and is therefore quite gloomy himself. I am what I am and I won't hide that. I will be sad when I have a reason to be and will smile at no one's jokes. I'll eat when I am hungry and not wait until it is convenient. I'll sleep when I am tired and will not serve anyone. I'll laugh when I am happy but will not flatter the whims of others.

Conrade   This is true, but you must reveal this part of your personality with some restraint. Since you have recently rebelled against your brother and he has just taken you back in his good graces, you need to choose the right time to allow your true self to be known.

Don John   I had rather be a canker in a hedge
than a rose in his grace, and it better fits my blood
to be disdain'd of all than to fashion a carriage to
30   rob love from any. In this (though I cannot be
said to be a flattering honest man) it must not be
denied but I am a plain-dealing villain. I am trusted
with a muzzle, and enfranchis'd with a clog, therefore
I have decreed not to sing in my cage. If I had my
35   mouth, I would bite; if I had my liberty, I would
do my liking. In the mean time let me be that I am,
and seek not to alter me.

Conrade   Can you make no use of your discontent?

Don John   I make all use of it, for I use it only.
40   Who comes here?

Enter **Borachio**.

What news, Borachio?

Borachio   I came yonder from a great supper. The
Prince your brother is royally entertain'd by Leonato,
and I can give you intelligence of an intended mar-
45   riage.

Don John   Will it serve for any model to build mischief on? What is he for a fool that betroths himself
to unquietness?

Borachio   Marry, it is your brother's right hand.

50   **Don John**   Who? the most exquisite Claudio?

Borachio   Even he.

Don John   A proper squire! And who, and who?
which way looks he?

Borachio   Marry, one Hero, the daughter and heir
55   of Leonato.

Don John   At this point, I would rather be a weed in a hedge than a rose in his garden. It fits my personality better to be disliked by all than to fabricate a way to garner love from anyone. Although I certainly am not a pleasing or sincere man, you have to admit that I am an unadorned and simple villain. They trust me as much as a muzzled dog and have given me as much freedom as a dog tied to a post. Because of this, I have promised myself not to be joyful. If I weren't muzzled, I would bite and if I were free, I would do as I please. In the meantime, however, leave me alone and don't try to change me.

Conrade   Is there some way that you can use this displeasure of yours?

Don John   I use it all the time; it is the only thing I use. Who's coming?

[**Borachio** *enters.*]

What's new, Borachio?

Borachio   I just came from an impressive dinner where your brother is being treated like royalty by Leonato, and I have news of a planned marriage.

Don John   Is it anything that I can cause trouble with? Who is the fool who wants to marry himself to disorder?

Borachio   It's your brother's right hand who wants to marry.

Don John   You mean the beautiful Claudio?

Borachio   Yes, he's the one.

Don John   Ah, such a handsome young man! And to whom is he directing his attentions?

Borachio   To Hero, the daughter and heir of Leonato.

Don John   A very forward March-chick! How
came you to this?

Borachio   Being entertain'd for a perfumer, as I was
smoking a musty room, comes me the Prince and
60   Claudio, hand in hand in sad conference. I whipt
me behind the arras, and there heard it agreed
upon that the Prince should woo Hero for himself, and having obtain'd her, give her to Count
64   Claudio.

Don John   Come, come, let us thither, this may
prove food to my displeasure. That young start-up
hath all the glory of my overthrow. If I can cross
him any way, I bless myself every way. You are
both sure, and will assist me?

70 **Conrade**   To the death, my lord.

Don John   Let us to the great supper, their cheer
is the greater that I am subdu'd. Would the cook
were a' my mind! Shall we go prove what's to be
done?

75 **Borachio**   We'll wait upon your lordship.

Exeunt.

Don John   She's precocious and very young! How did you learn about this?

Borachio   Employed as a perfumer, I was refreshing a musty room when the Prince and Claudio arrived in the midst of a serious conversation. I hid behind a screen and heard them agree upon a plan: that the Prince would woo Hero for himself and once he gained her approval, he would give her to Claudio.

Don John   Come on, let's go over there to the dance. This will help feed my anger. That young upstart takes glory in overthrowing me, and if I can disrupt his life in any way, I will be all the happier for it. Will you both help me?

Conrade   Until the day I die, my lord.

Don John   Okay, let's go to this elaborate supper; they will be happy to see that my mood has lightened. If only the cook thought the same way that I do. Shall we go see what has to be done?

Borachio   We'll follow you, lord.

[*They exit.*]

Act two

Scene 1

Enter **Leonato**, [**Antonio**] *his brother,* **Hero** *his daughter, and* **Beatrice** *his niece,* [**Margaret**, **Ursula**,] *and a* **Kinsman**.

Leonato   Was not Count John here at supper?

Antonio   I saw him not.

Beatrice   How tartly that gentleman looks! I never can see him but I am heart-burn'd an hour after.

5 **Hero**   He is of a very melancholy disposition.

Beatrice   He were an excellent man that were made just in the midway between him and Benedick: the one is too like an image and says nothing, and the other too like my lady's eldest son, evermore
10   tattling.

Leonato   Then half Signior Benedick's tongue in Count John's mouth, and half Count John's melancholy in Signior Benedick's face—

Beatrice   With a good leg and a good foot, uncle,
15   and money enough in his purse, such a man would win any woman in the world, if 'a could get her good will.

Leonato   By my troth, niece, thou wilt never get thee a husband, if thou be so shrewd of thy tongue.

20 **Antonio**   In faith, she's too curst.

Beatrice   Too curst is more than curst. I shall lessen God's sending that way, for it is said, "God sends a curst cow short horns—" but to a cow too curst he
24   sends none.

Act two

Scene 1

Enter **Leonato**, **Antonio**, **Hero**, **Beatrice**, *and others in a hallway inside Leonato's house.*

Leonato   Wasn't Don John at supper?

Antonio   I didn't see him.

Beatrice   That man looks so irritable! I have heartburn for an hour every time I see him.

Hero   He seems to have a very serious personality.

Beatrice   To combine half of him and half of Benedick would make an excellent example of a man; as it is, one is much like a painting and says nothing while the other is like a spoiled child who chatters incessantly.

Leonato   In other words, this man would be less talkative than Signior Benedick and less serious than Don John.

Beatrice   And if he were athletic, handsome, and wealthy this man could have any woman in the world as long as he could win her approval.

Leonato   Honestly, niece, you will never get a husband by speaking so harshly.

Antonio   I swear that she is too quarrelsome.

Beatrice   Too quarrelsome is more than just quarrelsome. If that is true I will decrease God's punishment according to the proverb that says, "God sends short horns to a quarrelsome cow, but sends none to a too quarrelsome cow."

Leonato   So, by being too curst, God will send you
no horns.

Beatrice   Just, if he send me no husband, for the
which blessing I am at him upon my knees every
29   morning and evening. Lord, I could not endure
a husband with a beard on his face, I had rather lie
in the woollen!

Leonato   You may light on a husband that hath no
beard.

Beatrice   What should I do with him? dress him
35   in my apparel, and make him my waiting-gentle-
woman? He that hath a beard is more than a youth,
and he that hath no beard is less than a man; and he
that is more than a youth is not for me, and he that
is less than a man, I am not for him; therefore I will
even take sixpence in earnest of the berrord, and
41   lead his apes into hell.

Leonato   Well then, go you into hell?

Beatrice   No, but to the gate, and there will the
devil meet me like an old cuckold, with horns on
45   his head, and say "Get you to heaven, Beatrice,
get you to heaven, here's no place for you maids."
So deliver I up my apes, and away to Saint Peter.
For the Heavens, he shows me where the bachelors
49   sit, and there live we as merry as the day is long.

Antonio   [*To Hero.*] Well, niece, I trust you will be
rul'd by your father.

Beatrice   Yes, faith, it is my cousin's duty to make
cur'sy and say "Father, as it please you." But
yet for all that, cousin, let him be a handsome fellow,
or else make another cur'sy and say "Father, as it
56   please me."

Leonato   Then, God will not send you horns because you are so quarrelsome?

Beatrice   Exactly. And I give thanks every morning and evening for the blessing of not having a husband. Sir, I couldn't tolerate a husband with a beard; in fact, I'd rather sleep with a scratchy wool blanket.

Leonato   Perhaps you will find a husband without a beard.

Beatrice   And what would I do with him? Dress him in my clothes and turn him into my maid? Should he have a beard, he is more than a boy, and without a beard he would not be a real man; but anyone who is older than a boy is not my type, and anyone who is not quite a man, well, I am not his type; so, I will take sixpence in pay from the bear trainer and lead his apes into hell, as they say.

Leonato   You mean you would rather go into hell?

Beatrice   No, only to the gate, where the cuckolded and horned devil will meet me and exclaim, "Go, Beatrice, get to heaven, this is no place for virgins," so I hand him the apes and off to Saint Peter's heavens I go. He shows me where the bachelors sit and there we all live happily ever after.

Antonio   [*to Hero*] Well, niece, I am sure that you will allow your father to make these decisions for you.

Beatrice   Yes, of course; it is my cousin's responsibility to obey her father's choice in a man and to say, "Father, as it pleases you." Except if he chooses a man that is not handsome, she will politely tell her father that she won't marry him and choose one herself.

Leonato   Well, niece, I hope to see you one day fitted
with a husband.

Beatrice   Not till God make men of some other
60   mettle than earth. Would it not grieve a woman
to be overmaster'd with a piece of valiant dust? to
make an account of her life to a clod of wayward
marl? No, uncle, I'll none. Adam's sons are my
brethren, and, truly I hold it a sin to match in my
65   kindred.

Leonato   Daughter, remember what I told you. If
the Prince do solicit you in that kind, you know
your answer.

Beatrice   The fault will be in the music, cousin, if
70   you be not woo'd in good time. If the Prince be
too important, tell him there is measure in every
thing, and so dance out the answer. For hear me,
Hero: wooing, wedding, and repenting, is as a
Scotch jig, a measure, and a cinquepace: the first
75   suit is hot and hasty, like a Scotch jig, and full
as fantastical; the wedding, mannerly-modest,
as a measure, full of state and ancientry; and then
comes repentance, and with his bad legs falls into
the cinquepace faster and faster, till he sink into
80   his grave.

Leonato   Cousin, you apprehend passing shrewdly.

Beatrice   I have a good eye, uncle, I can see a church
by daylight.

Leonato   The revellers are ent'ring, brother, make
85   good room.

[They put on their masks.]

62

Leonato   Well, niece, I hope to see you married one of these days.

Beatrice   I will not marry, not until God makes men out of something other than dirt. Can you imagine a woman being mastered over by a heroic piece of dust and having to report to a lump of clay? No, uncle, I won't marry; besides, Adam's sons are my brothers, and I believe that it is a sin to marry a relative.

Leonato   Daughter, remember what I told you: If the Prince asks you to marry him, you already know your answer.

Beatrice   Be certain, cousin, that he woos you properly. If he is too demanding, tell him that each stage of a romance is like a dance. Hero, the wooing, wedding, and repenting stages are like individual dances. The wooing is like a Scottish jig, passionate and fast; the wedding is like a dance performed before a King, slow, proper, and respectable; and then comes the repentance, a lively five-step dance, danced on bad legs, that speeds up faster and faster until the dancer falls over and dies.

Leonato   Cousin, you are extremely perceptive.

Beatrice   I have a good eye, uncle; I can see clearly in daylight.

Leonato   Our guests are arriving; let's give them plenty of room.

[*They all put on their masks.*]

Enter Prince **[Don] Pedro**, **Claudio**, *and* **Benedick**, *and*
[Don] John, *[and* **Borachio** *as maskers, with a Drum].*

Don Pedro   Lady, will you walk about with your
friend?

Hero   So you walk softly, and look sweetly, and
say nothing, I am yours for the walk, and especially
90   when I walk away.

Don Pedro   With me in your company?

Hero   I may say so when I please.

Don Pedro   And when please you to say so?

Hero   When I like your favor, for God defend
95   the lute should be like the case!

Don Pedro   My visor is Philemon's roof, within
the house is Jove.

Hero   Why then your visor should be thatch'd.

Don Pedro   Speak low if you speak love.

[They move aside.]

100   **Borachio**   Well, I would you did like me.

Margaret   So would not I for your own sake, for I
have many ill qualities.

Borachio   Which is one?

104   **Margaret**   I say my prayers aloud.

Borachio   I love you the better; the hearers may
cry amen.

[*Enter* **Don Pedro**, **Claudio**, **Benedick**, **Balthasar**, **Don John**, **Borachio**, **Margaret**, **Ursula**, *and others, masked.*]

Don Pedro   Lady, can I have this dance?

Hero   If you dance without stepping on my toes, are handsome, and don't speak, I would be happy to dance with you and remain with you after the dance.

Don Pedro   You will stay with me after the dance?

Hero   Yes, if I feel like it.

Don Pedro   When will you know if you feel like it?

Hero   That depends upon how I like your looks because God help us if your face looks worse than your mask.

Don Pedro   My mask is like Philemon's [*a poor man's*] simple thatched cottage where he entertained the god Jove [*king of Roman gods*], but my face is as handsome as Jove himself.

Hero   Well then, your mask should be bearded.

Don Pedro   Speak softly if you want to talk of love.

[*Don Pedro draws her aside; Borachio and Margaret move forward.*]

Borachio   Well, I wish that you liked me.

Margaret   It is better for you that I don't because I have many bad traits.

Borachio   Will you tell me one?

Margaret   I say my prayers out loud.

Borachio   That makes me love you all the more, and those who hear can answer, "Amen."

Margaret   God match me with a good dancer!

Borachio   Amen.

Margaret   And God keep him out of my sight when
110   the dance is done! Answer, clerk.

Borachio   No more words; the clerk is answer'd.

[*They move aside.*]

Ursula   I know you well enough, you are Signior
Antonio.

114 **Antonio**   At a word, I am not.

Ursula   I know you by the waggling of your head.

Antonio   To tell you true, I counterfeit him.

Ursula   You could never do him so ill-well, unless
you were the very man. Here's his dry hand up
and down. You are he, you are he.

120 **Antonio**   At a word, I am not.

Ursula   Come, come, do you think I do not know
you by your excellent wit? Can virtue hide itself?
Go to, mum, you are he. Graces will appear, and
there's an end.

[*They move aside.*]

125 **Beatrice**   Will you not tell me who told you so?

Benedick   No, you shall pardon me.

Beatrice   Nor will you not tell me who you are?

Benedick   Not now.

Margaret   God, please bring me a good dancer!

Borachio   Amen.

Margaret   And please God, take him away once the dance is over. You can answer "Amen" now, parish clerk.

Borachio   There is nothing more to say—the clerk has his answer.

[*Borachio and Margaret step aside, and Ursula and Antonio move forward.*]

Ursula   I know you too well, you are Signior Antonio.

Antonio   Seriously, no, I am not.

Ursula   I can tell it is you by the way you wiggle your head.

Antonio   No, honestly, I am just imitating him.

Ursula   The only way that you could imitate him so well is if you are him. Your hands are wrinkled like his; you are him.

Antonio   Seriously, no, I am not.

Ursula   Please, do you think that I wouldn't recognize your sense of humor, and is it possible for such an excellent virtue to remain hidden? Keep quiet, you are he, your virtues are apparent, and that's all there is to it.

[*Antonio and Ursula move aside, and Beatrice and Benedick move forward.*]

Beatrice   Tell me who told you that?

Benedick   No, you'll have to excuse me.

Beatrice   And you won't tell me who you are either?

Benedick   Not now.

Beatrice   That I was disdainful, and that I had my
good wit out of the "Hundred Merry Tales"—well,
131   this was Signior Benedick that said so.

Benedick   What's he?

Beatrice   I am sure you know him well enough.

Benedick   Not I, believe me.

135   **Beatrice**   Did he never make you laugh?

Benedick   I pray you, what is he?

Beatrice   Why, he is the Prince's jester, a very dull
fool; only his gift is in devising impossible slanders.
None but libertines delight in him, and the com-
140   mendation is not in his wit, but in his villainy,
for he both pleases men and angers them, and then
they laugh at him and beat him. I am sure he is in the
fleet; I would he had boarded me.

Benedick   When I know the gentleman, I'll tell him
145   what you say.

Beatrice   Do, do, he'll but break a comparison or
two on me, which peradventure, not mark'd, or not
laugh'd at, strikes him into melancholy, and then
there's a partridge wing sav'd, for the fool will eat
no supper that night. [*Music for the dance begins.*] We
151   must follow the leaders.

Benedick   In every good thing.

Beatrice   Nay, if they lead to any ill, I will leave
them at the next turning.

Dance. [Then] exeunt [all but Don John, Borachio, and Claudio].

Beatrice   Who said that I was contemptuous and that I get my sense of humor out of the joke book "Hundred Merry Tales"? Well, it had to be Signior Benedick.

Benedick   Who is that?

Beatrice   I am sure you know him well.

Benedick   No, I don't, believe me.

Beatrice   Did he ever make you laugh?

Benedick   Honestly, I do not know him.

Beatrice   Well, he is the Prince's jester and a very stupid fool at that. His only talent is inventing outrageous insults, and no one but the most immoral enjoy being with him. He is not known for his sense of humor but for his rudeness because he both pleases and angers at the same time; first people laugh at him, and then they beat him up. I am sure he is in the crowd somewhere; in fact, I think he tried to approach me.

Benedick   When I meet this man, I'll tell him what you've said.

Beatrice   Please do. He'll crack a joke or two about me and if no one laughs at it, he will get depressed and we'll have an extra partridge wing at supper because the fool will not eat that night. [*Music plays.*] Come, let's follow the leaders in the dance.

Benedick   We'll follow every good thing they do.

Beatrice   No, if they lead us to any trouble, I'll leave the floor at the next dance number.

[*Dance. Everyone exits except Don John, Borachio, and Claudio.*]

Don John   Sure my brother is amorous on Hero,
156   and hath withdrawn her father to break with him
about it. The ladies follow her, and but one visor
remains.

Borachio   And that is Claudio. I know him by his
160   bearing.

Don John   Are not you Signior Benedick?

Claudio   You know me well, I am he.

Don John   Signior, you are very near my brother
in his love. He is enamor'd on Hero. I pray you
dissuade him from her, she is no equal for his birth.
166   You may do the part of an honest man in it.

Claudio   How know you he loves her?

Don John   I heard him swear his affection.

Borachio   So did I too, and he swore he would marry
170   her to-night.

Don John   Come let us to the banquet.

Exeunt. Manet Claudio.

Claudio   Thus answer I in name of Benedick,
But hear these ill news with the ears of Claudio.
'Tis certain so, the Prince woos for himself.
175   Friendship is constant in all other things
Save in the office and affairs of love;
Therefore all hearts in love use their own tongues.
Let every eye negotiate for itself,
And trust no agent; for beauty is a witch
180   Against whose charms faith melteth into blood.
This is an accident of hourly proof,
Which I mistrusted not. Farewell therefore, Hero!

Enter **Benedick**.

Don John   Certainly my brother has wooed Hero and is now speaking with her father about it. The ladies are following her, but there is one man left with a mask.

Borachio   And that is Claudio: I can tell by the way he moves.

Don John   Aren't you Signior Benedick?

Claudio   You know me well; yes, I am Benedick.

Don John   Signior, you are close to my brother and know of his love for Hero. Please, try to discourage him from her because she is not equal to his rank. You would be doing him a great favor.

Claudio   How do you know that he loves her?

Don John   I heard him swear his affection for her.

Borachio   I did too, and he swore that he would marry her tonight.

Don John   Come on, let's go to the banquet.

[*Don John and Borachio exit.*]

Claudio   Although I said my name was Benedick, I heard this awful news with my own ears. It is true; the Prince is wooing Hero for himself. Friendship is sure in all things except when it comes to the business of love. Because of that, the one who loves must speak for himself and look out for his own interests. Don't trust anyone else to do it for you because beauty is a witch whose spells can turn trust into passion. This happens often, but I never suspected that it would happen to me. Good-bye, then, Hero!

[*Re-enter* **Benedick**.]

Benedick   Count Claudio?

Claudio   Yea, the same.

185 **Benedick**   Come, will you go with me?

Claudio   Whither?

Benedick   Even to the next willow, about your own
business, County. What fashion will you wear
the garland of? about your neck, like an usurer's
chain? or under your arm, like a lieutenant's scarf?
You must wear it one way, for the prince hath got

192   your Hero.

Claudio   I wish him joy of her.

Benedick   Why, that's spoken like an honest drovier;
so they sell bullocks. But did you think the Prince

196   would have serv'd you thus?

Claudio   I pray you leave me.

Benedick   Ho, now you strike like the blind man.
'Twas the boy that stole your meat, and you'll

200   beat the post.

Claudio   If it will not be, I'll leave you.

Exit.

Benedick   Alas, poor hurt fowl, now will he creep
into sedges. But that my Lady Beatrice should
know me, and not know me! The Prince's fool!
hah, it may be I go under that title because I am

206   merry. Yea, but so I am apt to do myself wrong.
I am not so reputed. It is the base (though bitter)
disposition of Beatrice that puts the world into her
person, and so gives me out. Well, I'll be reveng'd

210   as I may.

Benedick   Count Claudio?

Claudio   Yes, that's me.

Benedick   Come on, will you follow me?

Claudio   Where?

Benedick   Just over there to the next willow tree; it's in regard to your personal business, count. How are you going to wear your garland: around your neck like a money-lender's chain, or under your arm like a lieutenant's sash? You have to wear it one way or the other because the Prince has your Hero.

Claudio   I hope he enjoys her.

Benedick   My, don't you sound like a true cattle dealer— that's the way they sell their bulls. Do you honestly believe the Prince would treat you that way?

Claudio   Please, just go away.

Benedick   Wow! You are attacking me like a blind man who doesn't know who to attack. It was a thief that stole your meat, and you are striking out at the messenger.

Claudio   If you won't leave, I'll leave you.

[*He exits.*]

Benedick   Sad, the poor injured bird! Now he'll go hide in the bushes. I am surprised that my Lady Beatrice didn't know me, she should have. And to say that I am the Prince's fool! Ha! I may be called that because I am happy, but I shouldn't worry about it because I don't have the reputation of being a fool. It is because of Beatrice's vile and bitter personality that she describes me in this way, and she believes everyone else agrees with her. I'll get my revenge somehow.

Enter the Prince [**Don Pedro**]

Don Pedro   Now, signior, where's the Count? Did you see him?

Benedick   Troth, my lord, I have play'd the part of Lady Fame. I found him here as melancholy as a lodge in a warren. I told him, and I think I told him true, that your Grace had got the good will of this young lady, and I off'red him my company to a willow-tree, either to make him a garland, as being forsaken, or to bind him up a rod, as being worthy to be whipt.

216

Don Pedro   To be whipt! What's his fault?

Benedick   The flat transgression of a schoolboy, who being overjoy'd with finding a birds' nest, shows it his companion, and he steals it.

222

Don Pedro   Wilt thou make a trust a transgression? The transgression is in the stealer.

226

Benedick   Yet it had not been amiss the rod had been made, and the garland too, for the garland he might have worn himself, and the rod he might have bestow'd on you, who (as I take it) have stol'n his birds' nest.

231

Don Pedro   I will but teach them to sing, and restore them to the owner.

Benedick   If their singing answer your saying, by my faith you say honestly.

235

Don Pedro   The Lady Beatrice hath a quarrel to you. The gentleman that danc'd with her told her she is much wrong'd by you.

238

[**Don Pedro** *re-enters.*]

Don Pedro   Signior Benedick, where's the count? Did you see him?

Benedick   To be honest, my lord, I played the part of the gossip. I found him as depressed as a rabbit in a warren. I told him truthfully that you had earned the blessings of this young lady and offered to accompany him to the nearest willow tree, either to make a garland to be worn by an abandoned lover or to gather a bundle of rods worthy enough for his whipping.

Don Pedro   To be whipped! What did he do wrong?

Benedick   The simple wrongdoing of a schoolboy who is excited about finding a bird's nest, shows it to his friend, and the friend steals it.

Don Pedro   But is it wrong to trust? It is the thief who is wrong.

Benedick   It probably would have been wise to make both the garland and the rod; he could have worn the garland himself and used the rod to hit you because, as I under-stand, you have stolen his bird's nest.

Don Pedro   I only want to teach the nestlings to sing, and then I will return them to their rightful owner.

Benedick   If their responses agree with what you are saying, we will know that you are telling the truth.

Don Pedro   Lady Beatrice seems to be upset with you. She said that the gentleman she danced with told her that you insulted her.

Benedick   O, she misus'd me past the endurance of
a block; an oak but with one green leaf on it would
have answer'd her. My very visor began to assume
life, and scold with her. She told me, not thinking I had been myself, that I was the Prince's jester,
that I was duller than a great thaw, huddling jest
upon jest with such impossible conveyance upon
246   me that I stood like a man at a mark, with a
whole army shooting at me. She speaks poniards,
and every word stabs. If her breath were as terrible
as her terminations, there were no living near her,
she would infect to the north star. I would not
251   marry her, though she were endow'd with all
that Adam had left him before he transgress'd.
She would have made Hercules have turn'd spit,
yea, and have cleft his club to make the fire too.
Come, talk not of her; you shall find her the infernal
256   Ate in good apparel. I would to God some scholar
would conjure her, for certainly, while she is here,
a man may live as quiet in hell as in a sanctuary, and
people sin upon purpose, because they would go
thither; so indeed all disquiet, horror, and perturba-
261   tion follows her.

Enter **Claudio** *and* **Beatrice**, [**Leonato** *and* **Hero**].

Don Pedro   Look, here she comes.

Benedick   Will your grace command me any service
to the world's end? I will go on the slightest arrand
now to the Antipodes that you can devise to send
266   me on; I will fetch you a toothpicker now from
the furthest inch of Asia, bring you the length of
Prester John's foot, fetch you a hair off the great
Cham's beard, do you any embassage to the Pigmies,
rather than hold three words' conference with this
271   harpy. You have no employment for me?

Benedick   Oh, she has abused me so badly that even a
block of wood couldn't tolerate it. An oak tree with one
remaining leaf would be revived and want to respond to
her; even my mask seemed to come to life and argue with
her. She thought she was speaking to someone else and
told me that I was the Prince's jester and as dull as mud.
She piled insult upon insult against me and with such
speed and adeptness that I was stunned and felt as though I
was a targeted man with an entire army shooting at me.
Every word that she speaks stabs like a dagger, and if her
breath were as terrible as her comments there would be no
one living closer to her than the North Star. I wouldn't
marry her even if she possessed all the good qualities that
Adam had before he sinned. She would have forced Hercules to tend the roasting spit and to use his club to make
the fire. Please don't mention her name; you will see that
she is just like the goddess Ate [*who led men to rash
actions and ultimately ruin*], only well dressed. I pray to
God that a sorcerer will conjure her back to hell because
while she is here, hell, where people sin intentionally, is a
quiet sanctuary. By sending her back where she belongs, all
of the unrest, terror, and trouble will follow her.

Don Pedro   Look, here she comes.

[**Claudio**, **Beatrice**, **Hero**, *and* **Leonato** *enter.*]

Benedick   Do you have any small tasks for me on the other
side of the world? I will do anything that you can possibly
think of as far away as the Antipodes [*volcanic islands*]; I'll
get you a toothpick from the farthest regions of Asia, bring
a piece of Prester John's [*a Christian patriarch and king*]
foot, a hair from the great Kublai Khan's beard, or relay a
message to the Pigmies [*a race of dwarfs*], anything rather
than to have to say three words to this sharp-tongued
woman. Don't you have anything for me to do?

Don Pedro   None, but to desire your good company.

Benedick   O God, sir, here's a dish I love not, I can-
275   not endure my Lady Tongue.

Exit

Don Pedro   Come, lady, come, you have lost the
heart of Signior Benedick.

Beatrice   Indeed, my lord, he lent it me awhile, and
I gave him use for it, a double heart for his single
one. Marry, once before he won it of me with false
dice, therefore your Grace may well say I have
282   lost it.

Don Pedro   You have put him down, lady, you have
put him down.

Beatrice   So I would not he should do me, my lord,
286   lest I should prove the mother of fools. I have
brought Count Claudio, whom you sent me to seek.

Don Pedro   Why, how now, Count, wherefore are
you sad?

290   **Claudio**   Not sad, my lord.

Don Pedro   How then? sick?

Claudio   Neither, my lord.

Beatrice   The Count is neither sad, nor sick, nor
merry, nor well; but civil count, civil as an orange,
295   and something of that jealous complexion.

Don Pedro Not really, only that you keep me company.

Benedick Oh my God, sir, here's a dish that I do not like; I cannot stand my Lady Tongue.

[*Benedick exits.*]

Don Pedro Now, now, lady; you have lost Signior Benedick's heart.

Beatrice It sure looks that way, my lord. I borrowed it from him for awhile but paid interest for using it, a double heart for his single one. Truthfully, he won it from me in a dishonest dice game and so, yes, you might say that I have lost it.

Don Pedro You have put him down and completely humiliated him.

Beatrice I certainly hope that he doesn't put me down or I will surely have fools for children. Here is Count Claudio, whom you sent me to find.

Don Pedro Count! Why are you so sad?

Claudio I'm not sad, my lord.

Don Pedro What's the matter? Are you sick?

Claudio Neither, my lord.

Beatrice The count is not sad, sick, happy, or well, but he is civil. He is as Seville as an orange and appears to have a complexion similar in color to that of jealousy.

Don Pedro   I' faith, lady, I think your blazon to be
true, though, I'll be sworn, if he be so, his conceit
is false. Here, Claudio, I have woo'd in thy name,
and fair Hero is won. I have broke with her father,
and his good will obtain'd. Name the day of marriage,
301   and God give thee joy!

Leonato   Count, take of me my daughter, and with
her my fortunes. His grace hath made the match,
and all grace say amen to it.

305 **Beatrice**   Speak, Count, 'tis your cue.

Claudio   Silence is the perfectest herald of joy; I
were but little happy, if I could say how much!
Lady, as you are mine, I am yours: I give away
309   myself for you, and dote upon the exchange.

Beatrice   Speak, cousin, or (if you cannot) stop
his mouth with a kiss, and let not him speak neither.

Don Pedro   In faith, lady, you have a merry
heart.

Beatrice   Yea, my lord, I thank it—poor fool, it keeps
on the windy side of care. My cousin tells him in his
316   ear that he is in her heart.

Claudio   And so she doth, cousin.

Beatrice   Good Lord, for alliance! Thus goes every
one to the world but I, and I am sunburnt. I may
320   sit in a corner and cry "Heigh-ho for a husband!"

Don Pedro   Lady Beatrice, I will get you one.

Beatrice   I would rather have one of your father's
getting. Hath your Grace ne'er a brother like you?
Your father got excellent husbands, if a maid could
325   come by them.

Don Pedro   Honestly, lady, I believe that your perception is right on, though I would swear that if he is jealous, his notion is wrong. Claudio, here is Hero; I have spoken with her father and acquired his permission for marriage in your name. Name the wedding date and may God bring you much joy!

Leonato   Count, you have my permission to take my daughter and with her my fortunes. The Prince has composed this match, and may God say amen to it.

Beatrice   This is your cue to speak, count.

Claudio   My silence is my greatest declaration of joy. If I could say exactly how happy I am, I would be far less happy. Lady, just as you are mine, I am yours. I give myself to you and will cherish our exchange of love.

Beatrice   Cousin, say something; but if you cannot, kiss him so that he cannot speak either.

Don Pedro   Honestly, lady, you have a cheerful heart.

Beatrice   Yes, my lord, and I thank it, the poor fool, because it keeps me on the safe side of living. My cousin whispers to him in his ear that he is in her heart.

Claudio   And so she does, cousin.

Beatrice   Thank the Lord for marriage! So goes everyone in the world but me, because I am unattractive; I might just sit in a corner and sing "Heigh-ho for a husband!"

Don Pedro   Lady Beatrice, I will find you a husband.

Beatrice   I would rather have one of your father's sons. Do you have any brothers like you? Your father had sons who would make excellent husbands if only a girl could catch one.

Don Pedro   Will you have me, lady?

Beatrice   No, my lord, unless I might have another
for working-days. Your Grace is too costly to
wear every day. But I beseech your Grace pardon
330   me, I was born to speak all mirth and no matter.

Don Pedro   Your silence most offends me, and to
be merry best becomes you, for out a' question, you
were born in a merry hour.

Beatrice   No, sure, my lord, my mother cried, but
then there was a star danc'd, and under that was I born.
336   Cousins, God give you joy!

Leonato   Niece, will you look to those things I told
you of?

Beatrice   I cry you mercy, uncle. By your Grace's
340   pardon.

Exit Beatrice.

Don Pedro   By my troth, a pleasant-spirited lady.

Leonato   There's little of the melancholy element
in her, my Lord. She is never sad but when she sleeps,
and not ever sad then, for I have heard my daughter
say, she hath often dreamt of unhappiness, and wak'd
346   herself with laughing.

Don Pedro   She cannot endure to hear tell of a
husband.

Leonato   O, by no means, she mocks all her wooers
350   out of suit.

Don Pedro   She were an excellent wife for Benedick.

Leonato   O Lord, my lord, if they were but a week married,
they would talk themselves mad.

Don Pedro   Will you have me, lady?

Beatrice   No, my lord, not unless I could have another husband for the work week: You are too valuable to wear every day. Please forgive me, your grace; I was born to speak joyfully and of little substance.

Don Pedro   I would be offended if you were quiet, because your happiness becomes you; without a doubt, you were born at a joyous time.

Beatrice   Actually, my lord, my mother cried when I was born, but then a star danced in the sky and under that I was born. Cousins, God bring you joy!

Leonato   Niece, will you look to the things that we discussed?

Beatrice   Of course, please forgive me, uncle. Your grace, excuse me.

[*Beatrice exits.*]

Don Pedro   Honestly, she has such a pleasant personality.

Leonato   There's very little sadness in her spirit, my lord. The only time she is sad is when she sleeps, and she is not really sad then either. My daughter says that Beatrice often dreams of unhappiness and awakens with laughter.

Don Pedro   She cannot stand the thought of finding a husband.

Leonato   Definitely not. She ridicules all her suitors right out of their suits.

Don Pedro   She would be an excellent wife for Benedick.

Leonato   Oh, my Lord, if they were married they would make themselves crazy with talking in less than a week.

Don Pedro   County Claudio, when mean you to go
356   to church?

Claudio   To-morrow, my lord. Time goes on
crutches till love have all his rites.

Leonato   Not till Monday, my dear son, which is
hence a just sevennight, and a time too brief too, to
361   have all things answer my mind.

Don Pedro   Come, you shake the head at so long
a breathing, but I warrant thee, Claudio, the time
shall not go dully by us. I will in the interim under-
365   take one of Hercules' labors, which is, to
bring Signior Benedick and the Lady Beatrice into
a mountain of affection th' one with th' other. I
would fain have it a match, and I doubt not but to
fashion it, if you three will but minister such assist-
370   ance as I shall give you direction.

Leonato   My lord, I am for you, though it cost me
ten nights' watchings.

Claudio   And I, my lord.

Don Pedro   And you too, gentle Hero?

Hero   I will do any modest office, my lord, to help
376   my cousin to a good husband.

Don Pedro   Count Claudio, when do you want to set the date for the wedding?

Claudio   Tomorrow, my lord. Time will pass so slowly until our love is bound with a ceremony.

Leonato   Not until Monday, my dear son. That's only a week away and far too short a time to plan things as I would like.

Don Pedro   It's okay, Claudio. Even though you are restless at the wait, I promise that the time shall pass quickly for us. In the meantime, I want to undertake a Herculean task, which is to get Signior Benedick and Lady Beatrice to fall in love with each other. I would gladly see them together, and if you three will help when I ask, we can make this happen.

Leonato   My lord, I am with you in this although it will cost me my sleep for the next ten nights.

Claudio   I am with you too, my lord.

Don Pedro   And you, gentle Hero?

Hero   I will do anything I can to help my cousin find a good husband.

Don Pedro   And Benedick is not the unhopefullest
husband that I know. Thus far can I praise him: he is
of a noble strain, of approv'd valor, and confirm'd
380   honesty. I will teach you how to humor your
cousin, that she shall fall in love with Benedick, and I,
with your two helps, will so practice on Benedick
that, in despite of his quick wit and his queasy stomach, he shall fall in love with Beatrice. If we can do
385   this, Cupid is no longer an archer; his glory shall
be ours, for we are the only love-gods. Go in with
me, and I will tell you my drift.

Exeunt.

Scene 2

Enter **[Don] John** *and* **Borachio**.

Don John   It is so, the Count Claudio shall marry
the daughter of Leonato.

Borachio   Yea, my lord, but I can cross it.

Don John   Any bar, any cross, any impediment
5   will be med'cinable to me. I am sick in displeasure to him, and whatsoever comes athwart his affection ranges evenly with mine. How canst thou cross
this marriage?

Borachio   Not honestly, my lord; but so covertly that
10   no dishonesty shall appear in me.

Don John   Show me briefly how.

Don Pedro   And Benedick is not the worst of candidates for a husband that I have ever known. He is from a noble family and he is proven to be brave and honest. I will coach you in how to persuade your cousin that Benedick is in love with her and into falling in love with Benedick. With the two of you, we will do the same with Benedick despite his quick wit and distaste for marriage. He will fall in love with Beatrice. If we can pull this off, Cupid is no longer an archer; his fame will be ours, for we will be the only love gods. Let's go in and I will share my plan.

[*They all exit.*]

Scene 2

Enter **Don John** *and* **Borachio** *in Leonato's hallway.*

Don John   It is true; Count Claudio is going to marry Leonato's daughter.

Borachio   Yes, my lord, but I can prevent that from happening.

Don John   Anything that you can do to destroy this event would do wonders for me. I am so angry and disgusted with him that whatever will destroy his love will make me happy. How can you ruin this marriage?

Borachio   I'll have to lie to do it, my lord, but it will be done so secretively that I will not appear to be dishonest at all.

Don John   Briefly explain to me how.

Borachio   I think I told your lordship a year since,
how much I am in the favor of Margaret, the waiting-
gentlewoman to Hero.

15 **Don John**   I remember.

Borachio   I can, at any unseasonable instant of the
night, appoint her to look out at her lady's chamber-
window.

Don John   What life is in that, to be the death of
20   this marriage?

Borachio   The poison of that lies in you to temper.
Go you to the Prince your brother; spare not to tell
him that he hath wrong'd his honor in marrying the
renown'd Claudio—whose estimation do you mightily
hold up—to a contaminated stale, such a one as
26   Hero.

Don John   What proof shall I make of that?

Borachio   Proof enough to misuse the Prince, to vex
Claudio, to undo Hero, and kill Leonato. Look you
30   for any other issue?

Don John   Only to despite them, I will endeavour
any thing.

Borachio I think I told you how much Margaret, Hero's maid, has liked me for this past year.

Don John I remember.

Borachio I can, at any unseemly time at all during the night, ask her to meet me at her lady's bedroom window.

Don John How is that going to ruin the marriage?

Borachio How you do that is up to you. Go to your brother and tell him that he has made a grave mistake and ruined Claudio's honor (who you deeply respect) by arranging his marriage to such a low-class whore like Hero.

Don John And how am I going to prove that?

Borachio Your proof will be to deceive the Prince, torment Claudio, ruin Hero's reputation, and kill Leonato. Do you need any additional proof?

Don John To torture them, I will try anything.

Borachio   Go then, find me a meet hour to draw
Don Pedro and the Count Claudio alone, tell them
35   that you know that Hero loves me, intend a
kind of zeal both to the Prince and Claudio—
as in love of your brother's honor, who hath made
this match, and his friend's reputation, who is thus
like to be cozen'd with the semblance of a maid—
40   that you have discover'd thus. They will scarcely
believe this without trial. Offer them instances,
which shall bear no less likelihood than to see me
at her chamber-window, hear me call Margaret
Hero, hear Margaret term me Claudio; and bring
45   them to see this the very night before the intended wedding—for in the mean time I will so fashion
the matter that Hero shall be absent—and there shall
appear such seeming truth of Hero's disloyalty that
jealousy shall be call'd assurance, and all the prepara-
50   tion overthrown.

Don John   Grow this to what adverse issue it can,
I will put it in practice. Be cunning in the working
this, and thy fee is a thousand ducats.

Borachio   Be you constant in the accusation, and my
55   cunning shall not shame me.

Don John   I will presently go learn their day of
marriage.

Exeunt.

Borachio Find a good time to speak with Don Pedro and
Count Claudio alone. Tell them that you know that Hero
loves me. And speaking with great passion, tell them that
out of respect for your brother, whose honor will be com-
promised because he is responsible for the matchmaking,
and for his friend's reputation, which will be ruined if he
marries someone who is claiming to be a virgin, that you
have discovered otherwise. Of course they will not believe
this without proof. Bring them to witness this on the night
before the wedding. I will arrange to have Hero sleep else-
where, and what they will see at her bedroom window will
be me calling Margaret "Hero" and Margaret calling me
"Claudio." This will prove Hero's disloyalty and stir up such
jealousy that all of the preparations for the ceremony will
be brought down.

Don John Go ahead and arrange to follow through with the
plan, and I will do my part. If you are clever enough to carry
this out, I will pay you a thousand gold coins.

Borachio If you are serious about the accusations, my cleverness will not fail me.

Don John I'll go and try to find out the day of their
wedding.

[*They exit.*]

91

Scene 3

Enter **Benedick** *alone.*

Benedick   Boy!

[*Enter* **Boy**.]

Boy   Signior?

Benedick   In my chamber-window lies a book, bring
it hither to me in the orchard.

5   **Boy**   I am here already, sir.

Exit.

Benedick   I know that, but I would have thee hence,
and here again. I do much wonder that one man,
seeing how much another man is a fool when he
dedicates his behaviors to love, will, after he hath
10   laugh'd at such shallow follies in others, become
the argument of his own scorn by falling in love—
and such a man is Claudio. I have known when
there was no music with him but the drum and the
fife, and now had he rather hear the tabor and the
15   pipe; I have known when he would have walk'd
ten mile a-foot to see a good armor, and now will
he lie ten nights awake carving the fashion of a
new doublet; he was wont to speak plain and to the
purpose (like an honest man and a soldier), and now
20   is he turn'd orthography—his words are a very
fantastical banquet, just so many strange dishes.
May I be so converted and see with these eyes?
I cannot tell; I think not. I will not be sworn but
love may transform me to an oyster, but I'll take
25   my oath on it, till he have made [an] oyster of
me, he shall never make me such a fool. One woman
is fair, yet I am well; another is wise, yet I am

Scene 3

Enter **Benedick** *in Leonato's orchard.*

Benedick   Boy!

[*Enter* **Boy**.]

Boy   Signior?

Benedick   There is a book at my bedroom window: Bring it here to me.

Boy   I am already here, sir.

[*Exit Boy.*]

Benedick   I know that; but I want you to go there and back here again. It is a curious thing, how much one man derides and makes fun of another man who is in love and then turns around and does the same thing that he has ridiculed and falls in love; this is Claudio. I've known him when there were only the military sounds of the drum and fife, and now he would rather hear the dancing sounds of the tabor and pipe. There was a time when he would have walked ten miles on foot to see a good suit of armor, and now he lies awake for ten nights thinking about a new jacket. He used to speak clearly and to the point like an honest man and a soldier, but now he has become obsessive with fancy language. His words are like an artistic banquet with many unusual dishes. Will the same thing happen to me? I cannot tell; I don't think so, although I won't swear to it. Love might transform me into an oyster, but I will swear that until love has made an oyster of me, he will never turn me into a fool. A beautiful woman approaches and I am not enthused; another woman who is honorable and another who is wise

well; another virtuous, yet I am well; but till all
graces be in one woman, one woman shall not come
30   in my grace. Rich she shall be, that's certain;
wise, or I'll none; virtuous, or I'll never cheapen
her; fair, or I'll never look on her; mild, or come
not near me; noble, or not I for an angel; of good
discourse, an excellent musician, and her hair shall
35   be of what color it please God. Ha! the Prince
and Monsieur Love. I will hide me in the arbor.

[*Withdraws.*]

Enter Prince [**Don Pedro**], **Leonato, Claudio.** *Music*
[*within*].

Don Pedro   Come, shall we hear this music?

Claudio   Yea, my good lord. How still the evening
is,
As hush'd on purpose to grace harmony!

Don Pedro   See you where Benedick hath hid him-
40   self?

Claudio   O, very well, my lord. The music ended,
We'll fit the [hid]-fox with a pennyworth.

Enter **Balthasar** *with Music.*

Don Pedro   Come, Balthasar, we'll hear that song
again.

Balthasar   O good my lord, tax not so bad a voice
45   To slander music any more than once.

Don Pedro   It is the witness still of excellency
To put a strange face on his own perfection.
I pray thee sing, and let me woo no more.

appear and I still remain indifferent. Only until I meet one woman who has all three characteristics will I be per-suaded. She must be wealthy for sure; wise and honest, or I'll never bargain for her; beautiful, or I'll never look at her. She must be mild mannered or don't bother to come near me; noble, or I won't have her even if she is an angel. She must speak well, be an excellent musician, and her hair should be of whatever color that pleases God. Look! It's the Prince and Mr. Love! I'll hide in the trees.

[*Benedick hides.*]

[*Enter* **Don Pedro**, **Claudio**, *and* **Leonato**.]

Don Pedro   Come on, let's listen to some music.

Claudio   Yes, my good lord. The evening seems to be inten-tionally still and perfect for music.

Don Pedro   [*whispering to Claudio*] Did you see where Benedick is hiding?

Claudio   [*whispering to Don Pedro*] Yes I did, my lord, and once the music ends, we will give the hidden fox more than he bargained for.

[*Enter* **Balthasar** *with Music.*]

Don Pedro   Come, Balthasar, let's hear that song again.

Balthasar   Oh please, my lord, don't ask a bad voice to insult a song more than once.

Don Pedro   It is a sign of excellence when someone pre-tends not to know his own perfection. Please, don't make me woo you; sing.

Balthasar   Because you talk of wooing, I will sing,
50   Since many a wooer doth commence his suit
To her he thinks not worthy, yet he woos,
Yet will he swear he loves.

Don Pedro   Nay, pray thee come,
Or if thou wilt hold longer argument,
Do it in notes.

Balthasar   Note this before my notes:
There's not a note of mine that's worth the noting.

Don Pedro   Why, these are very crotchets that he
56   speaks—
Note notes, forsooth, and nothing.

[*Air.*]

Benedick   Now, divine air! now is his soul ravish'd!
Is it not strange that sheep's guts should hale souls
out of men's bodies? Well, a horn for my money
61   when all's done.

THE SONG

Balthasar

Sigh no more, ladies, sigh no more,
    Men were deceivers ever,
One foot in sea, and one on shore,
65   To one thing constant never.
Then sigh not so, but let them go,
    And be you blithe and bonny,
Converting all your sounds of woe
    Into hey nonny nonny.
70   Sing no more ditties, sing no moe,
    Of dumps so dull and heavy;
The fraud of men was ever so,
    Since summer first was leavy.
Then sigh not so, etc.

96

Balthasar   Because I don't want you to woo me, I will sing. But you are like a suitor who woos a woman even though he thinks she is unworthy, yet he continues to woo and swears he loves her.

Don Pedro   Please, sing now. Or if you want to argue any longer do it in a song.

Balthasar   But what you need to know before I sing my notes is that there's not a note of mine that is worth noting.

Don Pedro   What strange ideas he is speaking of; note, notes, in truth he is speaking of nothing.

[*Music plays.*]

Benedick   Listen! A beautiful melody. Now his soul is enchanted! Isn't it strange how the sounds that come from strings seem to pull men's souls from their bodies? When all is said and done, I'd rather listen to a horn.

The Song

Balthasar

Sigh no more, ladies, sigh no more,
Men were deceivers ever,
One foot in sea and one on shore,
To one thing constant never:
Then sigh not so, but let them go,
And be you blithe and bonny,
Converting all your sounds of woe
Into Hey nonny, nonny.
Sing no more ditties, sing no moe,
Of dumps so dull and heavy;
The fraud of men was ever so,
Since summer first was leafy:
Then sigh not so . . .

75 **Don Pedro**   By my troth, a good song.

Balthasar   And an ill singer, my lord.

Don Pedro   Ha, no, no, faith, thou sing'st well
enough for a shift.

Benedick   An he had been a dog that should have
80 howl'd thus, they would have hang'd him, and
I pray God his bad voice bode no mischief. I had as
live have heard the night-raven, come what plague
could have come after it.

Don Pedro   Yea, marry, dost thou hear, Balthasar?
85 I pray thee get us some excellent music; for
to-morrow night we would have it at the Lady Hero's
chamber-window.

Balthasar   The best I can, my lord.

Exit Balthasar.

Don Pedro   Do so, farewell. Come hither, Leonato.
What was it you told me of to-day, that your niece
91 Beatrice was in love with Signior Benedick?

Claudio   [*Aside.*] O, ay, stalk on, stalk on, the
fowl sits.—I did never think that lady would have
94 lov'd any man.

Leonato   No, nor I neither, but most wonderful that
she should so dote on Signior Benedick, whom she
hath in all outward behaviors seem'd ever to abhor.

Benedick   Is't possible? Sits the wind in that corner?

Leonato   By my troth, my lord, I cannot tell what to
think of it but that she loves him with an enrag'd af-
101 fection; it is past the infinite of thought.

Don Pedro   May be she doth but counterfeit.

Don Pedro   Truly, that is a good song.

Balthasar   But not such a great singer, my lord.

Don Pedro   No, no, please, you sing well enough to make do.

Benedick   [*aside*] If he had been a dog that howled like that, they would have hung him. I pray to God that his bad voice isn't an omen for something dreadful. I would just have gladly heard the night raven even if it would be followed by the plague.

Don Pedro   Yes, Balthasar, do you hear me? Please find some excellent music for tomorrow night because we want to serenade Hero at her bedroom window.

Balthasar   I will do the best that I can, my lord.

Don Pedro   Please do; good-bye.

[*Balthasar exits.*]

Come here, Leonato. What was it that you told me today about your niece Beatrice being in love with Signior Benedick?

Claudio   Oh, yes. [*aside to Don Pedro*] Keep tracking, keep tracking, our prey is close by.—I didn't think she was capable of loving any man.

Leonato   No, neither did I. It is wonderful that she seems to adore Signior Benedick, but from the way she acts, she seems to hate him.

Benedick   [*aside*] Is it possible? Is that what's happening, am I hearing correctly?

Leonato   Honestly, my lord, I don't know what to think, but the fact that she passionately loves him is beyond thinking.

Don Pedro   Maybe she is merely pretending.

Claudio   Faith, like enough.

Leonato   O God! counterfeit? There was never
counterfeit of passion came so near the life of passion
106   as she discovers it.

Don Pedro   Why, what effects of passion shows she?

Claudio   [*Aside.*]. Bait the hook well, this fish will
bite.

Leonato   What effects, my lord? She will sit you—
111   you heard my daughter tell you how.

Claudio   She did indeed.

Don Pedro   How, how, I pray you? You amaze
me, I would have thought her spirit had been in-
115   vincible against all assaults of affection.

Leonato   I would have sworn it had, my lord,
especially against Benedick.

Benedick   I should think this a gull, but that the white-
bearded fellow speaks it. Knavery cannot sure hide
120   himself in such reverence.

Claudio   [*Aside.*] He hath ta'en th' infection. Hold
it up.

Don Pedro   Hath she made her affection known to
Benedick?

Leonato   No, and swears she never will. That's her
126   torment.

Claudio   'Tis true indeed, so your daughter says.
"Shall I," says she, "that have so oft encount'red him
129   with scorn, write to him that I love him?"

Claudio   Honestly, that is likely.

Leonato   Oh God, pretending! If she is pretending, no one could do it with such passion and make it appear so heartfelt.

Don Pedro   Why, what kinds of passion does she demonstrate?

Claudio   [*aside to Leonato*] Bait the hook well; this fish is going to bite.

Leonato   What kind of passion? She will take a seat, you heard my daughter tell you how.

Claudio   Yes, she did.

Don Pedro   How, how, will you tell me please? This is amazing; I would have guessed that her personality would be unconquerable against all signs of affection.

Leonato   I would have sworn it, too, my lord, especially toward Benedick.

Benedick   [*aside*] I should think that this is a trick, except the white-bearded fellow is saying it, and trickery cannot hide behind such a respectable person.

Claudio   [*aside to Don Pedro*] He has caught the disease; keep it up.

Don Pedro   Has she told Benedick that she likes him yet?

Leonato   No, and she swears that she never will and it is tormenting her.

Claudio   That's true, and your daughter says that Beatrice questions whether or not she should write to him "and tell him that I love him even though I've treated him discourteously."

Leonato   This says she now when she is beginning to write to him, for she'll be up twenty times
a night, and there will she sit in her smock till she
have writ a sheet of paper. My daughter tells us all.

Claudio   Now you talk of a sheet of paper, I re-
135   member a pretty jest your daughter told [us of].

Leonato   O, when she had writ it, and was reading it
over, she found "Benedick" and "Beatrice" between
the sheet?

139 **Claudio**   That.

Leonato   O, she tore the letter into a thousand half-
pence; rail'd at herself, that she should be so im-
modest to write to one that she knew would flout
her. "I measure him," says she, "by my own spirit,
for I should flout him, if he writ to me, yea, though
145   I love him, I should."

Claudio   Then down upon her knees she falls,
weeps, sobs, beats her heart, tears her hair, prays,
curses: "O sweet Benedick! God give me pa-
149   tience!"

Leonato   She doth indeed, my daughter says so; and
the ecstasy hath so much overborne her that my
daughter is sometime afeared she will do a desperate
outrage to herself. It is very true.

Don Pedro   It were good that Benedick knew of it
155   by some other, if she will not discover it.

Claudio   To what end? he would make but a sport
of it, and torment the poor lady worse.

Don Pedro   An he should, it were an alms to hang
him. She's an excellent sweet lady, and (out of all
160   suspicion) she is virtuous.

Leonato   She says this when she begins to write. She'll be up twenty times a night, sitting there in her slip until she has written a full page. My daughter told us this.

Claudio   Now that you mention a sheet of paper, I remember a funny story that Hero told us.

Leonato   Oh, you mean when Hero found the page and discovered that it had "Benedick" and "Beatrice" written all over it?

Claudio   That's the one.

Leonato   Oh, she ripped the letter into a thousand pieces and scolded herself for being so bold as to try to write someone that she knows would make a fool of her. She says, "I measure him by my own personality, and I would certainly make a fool of him if he wrote to me. Yes, but I love him, so I should write to him."

Claudio   And then she falls to her knees and begins to cry and sob, and then beats her heart, tears her hair out, prays, and curses: "Oh sweet Benedick! God give me patience!"

Leonato   She did, honestly, my daughter said so. This madness has overwhelmed her so deeply that Hero is afraid that she will do something desperate to herself. That is very true.

Don Pedro   It would be good if someone told Benedick without her knowing it.

Claudio   What for? He would only make fun of it and torment her even more.

Don Pedro   If he did that it would be considered a cause to hang him. She's a very sweet lady, beyond suspicion and honorable.

Claudio   And she is exceeding wise.

Don Pedro   In every thing but in loving Benedick.

Leonato   O my lord, wisdom and blood combat-
164   ing in so tender a body, we have ten proofs to
one that blood hath the victory. I am sorry for
her, as I have just cause, being her uncle and her
guardian.

Don Pedro   I would she had bestow'd this dotage
on me, I would have daff'd all other respects, and
made her half myself. I pray you tell Benedick of
171   it, and hear what 'a will say.

Leonato   Were it good, think you?

Claudio   Hero thinks surely she will die, for she
says she will die if he love her not, and she will die
ere she make her love known, and she will die if he
woo her, rather than she will bate one breath of her
177   accustom'd crossness.

Don Pedro   She doth well. If she should make
tender of her love, 'tis very possible he'll scorn it,
for the man (as you know all) hath a contemptible
181   spirit.

Claudio   He is a very proper man.

Don Pedro   He hath indeed a good outward happiness.

Claudio   Before God, and in my mind, very wise.

Don Pedro   He doth indeed show some sparks that
187   are like wit.

Claudio   And I take him to be valiant.

Claudio   And she is extremely intelligent.

Don Pedro   In every thing, except loving Benedick.

Leonato   Oh, my lord, when wisdom and passion go against each other in someone so young, it is a ten to one chance that passion will win. I feel sorry for her and rightfully so, because I am her uncle and her guardian.

Don Pedro   I wish she would have given me this affection. I would have put aside all other possibilities and made her my wife. I beg you, please tell Benedick of it and listen to what he has to say.

Leonato   Do you think that's a good idea?

Claudio   Hero thinks that she will surely die because Beatrice says that she will die if he doesn't love her, and she will die if she doesn't tell him about her love for him, and she will die if he woos her and she has to hold back any of her usual insults.

Don Pedro   She is probably right. If she should offer him her love, it is possible that he will scorn it because we all know that he has a contemptuous personality.

Claudio   He is a very handsome man.

Don Pedro   He is fortunate to be attractive and suitable.

Claudio   I swear to God that he is very wise.

Don Pedro   He definitely shows signs of having a sense of humor.

Claudio   And I know that he is courageous.

Don Pedro   As Hector, I assure you, and in the
managing of quarrels you may say he is wise, for
either he avoids them with great discretion, or under-
192   takes them with a most Christian-like fear.

Leonato   If he do fear God, 'a must necessarily keep
peace; if he break the peace, he ought to enter into
195   a quarrel with fear and trembling.

Don Pedro   And so will he do, for the man doth
fear God, howsoever it seems not in him by some
large jests he will make. Well, I am sorry for your
niece. Shall we go seek Benedick, and tell him of
200   her love?

Claudio   Never tell him, my lord. Let her wear it
out with good counsel.

Leonato   Nay, that's impossible, she may wear her
heart out first.

Don Pedro   Well, we will hear further of it by
206   your daughter, let it cool the while. I love
Benedick well, and I could wish he would modestly
examine himself, to see how much he is unworthy
so good a lady.

Leonato   My lord, will you walk? Dinner is ready.

Claudio   [*Aside.*] If he do not dote on her upon
212   this, I will never trust my expectation.

Don Pedro   [*Aside.*] Let there be the same net
spread for her, and that must your daughter and
215   her gentlewomen carry. The sport will be, when
they hold one an opinion of another's dotage, and no
such matter; that's the scene that I would see, which
will be merely a dumb show. Let us send her to call
him in to dinner.

[*Exeunt Don Pedro, Claudio, and Leonato.*]

Don Pedro   As brave as Hector (a Grecian hero of Troy), I know. You can also say that he is sensible when dealing with arguments because he either avoids them all together or accepts them with a great Christian-like apprehension.

Leonato   If he does fear God, he must keep peace by necessity, and if he breaks the peace, he should enter into an argument with fear and trembling.

Don Pedro   And that is what he would do because he is a God-fearing man, although you wouldn't think so by some of the jokes he makes. But I am sorry for your niece. Should we go find Benedick and tell him of Beatrice's love?

Claudio   No, never tell him, let her figure it out with the help of some good advice.

Leonato   No, that's impossible. She will wear her heart out first.

Don Pedro   Well, let's discuss it further with your daughter and leave it alone for awhile. I love Benedick, but I wish that he would take a modest look at himself and see how unworthy he is of this good lady.

Leonato   My lord, shall we be going? Dinner is ready.

Claudio   [*Aside*] If he does not fall for her after this, I will never trust my intuition.

Don Pedro   The same snare should be set for Beatrice as well. Your daughter and her maid will carry it out. But the fun part will be when both Beatrice and Benedick believe that the other is in love with them, when none of it is true. That's what I want to see; it will be a pantomime because they both will be speechless. Let's send Beatrice out to call him to dinner.

[*Don Pedro, Claudio, and Leonato exit.*]

Benedick   [*Coming forward.*] This can be no trick:
221   the conference was sadly borne; they have
the truth of this from Hero; they seem to pity the
lady. It seems her affections have their full bent.
Love me? why, it must be requited. I hear how
I am censur'd; they say I will bear myself proudly,
if I perceive the love come from her; they say too
227   that she will rather die than give any sign of
affection. I did never think to marry. I must not
seem proud; happy are they that hear their detrac-
tions, and can put them to mending. They say the
lady is fair; 'tis a truth, I can bear them witness;
232   and virtuous; 'tis so, I cannot reprove it; and
wise, but for loving me; by my troth, it is no addition to her wit, nor no great argument of her folly,
for I will be horribly in love with her. I may chance
have some odd quirks and remnants of wit broken
on me, because I have rail'd so long against marriage;
238   but doth not the appetite alter? A man loves
the meat in his youth that he cannot endure in his
age. Shall quips and sentences and these paper
bullets of the brain awe a man from the career of
his humor? No, the world must be peopled. When
243   I said I would die a bachelor, I did not think
I should live till I were married. Here comes Beatrice.
By this day, she's a fair lady. I do spy some marks of
love in her.

Enter **Beatrice**.

Beatrice   Against my will I am sent to bid you come
248   in to dinner.

Benedick   Fair Beatrice, I thank you for your pains.

Benedick [*coming forward*] This cannot be a trick: They were speaking with such seriousness and they have Hero's word. They seem to feel sorry for her, and it appears that they are sincerely concerned about Beatrice's affections. She loves me! I have to love her back. They say that I will be haughty if I am aware that she loves me, and they also say that she would rather die than give any sign of affection. I never thought about marriage. I must not appear to be haughty. I am happy to hear of my faults and try to change my old ways. They say she is beautiful, that is true and I agree with them; and honorable, that's true and I cannot disprove that; and she is smart, except for loving me. Truthfully, that is no proof of her intelligence nor is it substance for her foolishness, because I will be horribly in love with her. I may possibly have some quibbles and jokes played on me because I have been against marriage for so long, but can't opinions change? A man might love meat in his youth but cannot stand it in his old age. Should these quips and statements and these paper bullets of the brain cause someone to veer from his chosen path? No, the world needs to be populated. When I said that I would die a bachelor, I didn't think I would live until I was married. Here comes Beatrice. By God! She is a beautiful lady. I do see some evidence of love in her.

[*Enter* **Beatrice**.]

Beatrice Against my wishes, I have been sent here to ask you to come in to dinner.

Benedick Beautiful Beatrice, thank you for your efforts.

Beatrice   I took no more pains for those thanks
than you take pains to thank me. If it had been
252   painful, I would not have come.

Benedick   You take pleasure then in the message?

Beatrice   Yea, just so much as you may take upon
a knive's point, and choke a daw withal. You have
256   no stomach, signior, fare you well.

Exit.

Benedick   Ha! "Against my will I am sent to bid
you come in to dinner"—there's a double meaning
in that. "I took no more pains for those thanks
than you took pains to thank me"—that's as much
as to say, "Any pains that I take for you is as easy
262   as thanks." If I do not take pity of her, I am
a villain; if I do not love her, I am a Jew. I will go
get her picture.

Exit.

Beatrice   Actually, I made no more effort for those thanks than you make the effort to thank me. If it had been too much effort, I wouldn't have come.

Benedick   Then you are happy to bring the message?

Beatrice Yes, just as much as you might be at choking a bird at knifepoint. You're not hungry, Signior, so good-bye.

[*Beatrice exits.*]

Benedick   Ha! "Against my wishes I am sent to ask you to come in to dinner"—there's a double meaning in that. And, "I made no more effort for those thanks than you make the effort to thank me." That's just like saying any effort that I take for you is as easy as thanks. I am a scoundrel if I do not feel sorry for her; if I do not love her, I am cruel. I will go get her picture.

[*Benedick exits.*]

Act three

Scene 1

Enter **Hero** *and two gentlewomen,* **Margaret** *and* **Ursley.**★

Hero   Good Margaret, run thee to the parlor,
There shalt thou find my cousin Beatrice
Proposing with the Prince and Claudio.
Whisper her ear, and tell her I and Ursley
5   Walk in the orchard, and our whole discourse
Is all of her. Say that thou overheardst us,
And bid her steal into the pleached bower,
Where honeysuckles, ripened by the sun,
Forbid the sun to enter, like favorites
10   Made proud by princes, that advance their pride
Against that power that bred it. There will she hide her,
To listen our propose. This is thy office;
Bear thee well in it, and leave us alone.

Margaret   I'll make her come, I warrant you, presently.

[*Exit.*]

15 **Hero**   Now, Ursula, when Beatrice doth come,
As we do trace this alley up and down,
Our talk must only be of Benedick.
When I do name him, let it be thy part
To praise him more than ever man did merit.
20   My talk to thee must be how Benedick
Is sick in love with Beatrice. Of this matter
Is little Cupid's crafty arrow made,
That only wounds by hearsay.

Enter **Beatrice** [*behind*].

Now begin,
For look where Beatrice like a lapwing runs
25   Close by the ground, to hear our conference.

112   ★Variant form of Ursula

Act three

Scene 1

Enter **Hero**, **Margaret**, *and* **Ursula** *in Leonato's garden.*

Hero   Margaret, please run into the parlor where Beatrice is talking to the Prince and Claudio. Whisper to her that you overheard Ursula and I having a discussion about her while walking in the orchard. Tell her that she can listen to the conversation by hiding in the arbor where the boughs of blooming honeysuckle intertwine and shade the path that was once a favorite place of indulged princes who schemed against the royalty who created them. This is your job. Do it well and then leave us alone.

Margaret   I'll make her come immediately, I promise you.

[*Margaret exits.*]

Hero   Now, Ursula, when Beatrice arrives, as we are walking back and forth on the covered path, we can only talk about Benedick. When I mention his name, your part will be to praise him excessively. What I'll say to you is how Benedick is madly in love with Beatrice. We are making arrows the same way that Cupid does but instead they wound with gossip and rumors.

[**Beatrice** *enters behind the arbor.*]

Let's begin: Look how Beatrice follows us bent close to the ground like a long-legged plover anxious to hear our conversation.

Ursula   The pleasant'st angling is to see the fish
Cut with her golden oars the silver stream,
And greedily devour the treacherous bait;
So angle we for Beatrice, who even now
30 Is couched in the woodbine coverture.
Fear you not my part of the dialogue.

Hero   Then go we near her, that her ear lose nothing
Of the false sweet bait that we lay for it.

[They advance to the bower.]

No, truly, Ursula, she is too disdainful,
35 I know her spirits are as coy and wild
As haggards of the rock.

Ursula   But are you sure
That Benedick loves Beatrice so entirely?

Hero   So says the Prince and my new-trothed lord.

Ursula   And did they bid you tell her of it, madam?

Hero   They did entreat me to acquaint her of it,
41 But I persuaded them, if they lov'd Benedick,
To wish him wrastle with affection,
And never to let Beatrice know of it.

Ursula   Why did you so? Doth not the gentleman
45 Deserve as full as fortunate a bed
As ever Beatrice shall couch upon?

Ursula [*aside to Hero*] The best thing about fishing is seeing the fish hurrying through the stream and greedy to eat the deceiving bait. We are fishing for Beatrice, who right now is cowering behind the bower. Don't worry; I'll play my part in the conversation.

Hero [*aside to Ursula*] Let's go closer to her so that she can hear everything of this false but sweet bait that we are laying out for her.

[*They approach the bower.*]

No, honestly, Ursula, she is too contemptuous; I know that her personality is as aloof and rebellious as wild hawks on a cliff.

Ursula But are you sure that Benedick loves Beatrice so much?

Hero Yes, the Prince and my fiancé both say so.

Ursula Did they ask you to tell Beatrice?

Hero Yes, they begged me to tell her, but I told them that if they loved Benedick that they should advise him to struggle with his emotions and to never let Beatrice know.

Ursula Why did you say that? Doesn't Benedick deserve a mate as good as Beatrice should have?

Hero   O god of love! I know he doth deserve
As much as may be yielded to a man;
But nature never fram'd a woman's heart
50   Of prouder stuff than that of Beatrice.
Disdain and scorn ride sparkling in her eyes,
Misprising what they look on, and her wit
Values itself so highly that to her
All matter else seems weak. She cannot love,
55   Nor take no shape nor project of affection,
She is so self-endeared.

Ursula   Sure I think so;
And therefore certainly it were not good
She knew his love, lest she'll make sport at it.

Hero   Why, you speak truth. I never yet saw man,
How wise, how noble, young, how rarely featur'd,
61   But she would spell him backward. If fair-fac'd,
She would swear the gentleman should be her sister;
If black, why, Nature, drawing of an antic,
Made a foul blot; if tall, a lance ill-headed;
65   If low, an agot very vildly cut;
If speaking, why, a vane blown with all winds;
If silent, why, a block moved with none.
So turns she every man the wrong side out,
And never gives to truth and virtue that
70   Which simpleness and merit purchaseth.

Ursula   Sure, sure, such carping is not commendable.

Hero   Oh god of love! I know that he deserves as much as could be given to a man, but nature never built any woman's heart more proud than Beatrice's. Contempt and scorn sparkle in her eyes, which despise everything they see. She values her cleverness and ability to speak with such sharpness or humor so highly that whatever anyone else says is weak in comparison. She cannot love or even begin to know what it is to give affection because she is so self-absorbed.

Ursula   Of course, I agree. It is not good for her to know that Benedick loves her, otherwise she would laugh at it.

Hero   You're right. If a man were wise, decent, young, and good-looking, she would turn all of his merits into faults. If he were handsome, she would say that the gentleman should be her sister; if he were dark-skinned, she would say that nature had made a horrible inkblot error while drawing a misshaped form. If he were tall, he'd be a large-headed spear; if short, an agate that was a poorly carved miniature; if the man should speak, he'd be a weather vane blowing in all directions, and if silent, a piece of wood that was incapable of being moved. She turns every man she meets inside out and never acknowledges the honesty, virtue, and sincerity that he deserves.

Ursula   Such mockery is not an admirable trait, that's for certain.

Hero   No, not to be so odd, and from all fashions,
As Beatrice is, cannot be commendable.
But who dare tell her so? If I should speak,
She would mock me into air; O, she would laugh me
76   Out of myself, press me to death with wit.
Therefore let Benedick, like cover'd fire,
Consume away in sighs, waste inwardly.
It were a better death than die with mocks,
80   Which is as bad as die with tickling.

Ursula   Yet tell her of it, hear what she will say.

Hero   No, rather I will go to Benedick,
And counsel him to fight against his passion,
And truly I'll devise some honest slanders
85   To stain my cousin with. One doth not know
How much an ill word may empoison liking.

Ursula   O, do not do your cousin such a wrong.
She cannot be so much without true judgment—
Having so swift and excellent a wit
90   As she is priz'd to have—as to refuse
So rare a gentleman as Signior Benedick.

Hero   He is the only man of Italy,
Always excepted my dear Claudio.

Ursula   I pray you be not angry with me, madam,
95   Speaking my fancy: Signior Benedick,
For shape, for bearing, argument and valor,
Goes foremost in report through Italy.

Hero   Indeed he hath an excellent good name.

Ursula   His excellence did earn it, ere he had it.
100   When are you married, madam?

Hero   No, behavior that is so peculiar and abnormal cannot be commendable. But who would dare tell her this? If I told her, she would chastise me until I disappeared into the air, or laugh me out of my body, or kill me with her wit. Benedick will have to stifle his desires like a smothered fire and waste away inwardly. It's a better way to die than to be mocked to death, which is as bad as being tickled to death.

Ursula   Maybe you should tell her and hear what she has to say.

Hero   No, I'd rather go to Benedick and advise him to fight against his passion. I'll invent some truthful insults to tarnish my cousin's reputation. You never know how much an unkind word will do to discourage affection.

Ursula   Oh, don't do such a mean thing to your cousin. She really can't be that lacking in good judgment—with her prized intelligence, how could she refuse a gentleman like Signior Benedick, who is a rare find?

Hero   He is the very best man in Italy, except for my dear Claudio.

Ursula   Please don't be angry with me for speaking my mind, but Signior Benedick is widely considered to be the best man in Italy for his looks, character, ability to converse, and courageousness.

Hero   Yes, he has an excellent reputation.

Ursula   He's earned his excellent reputation although he had it before he earned it. When are you to be married, madam?

Hero   Why, every day to-morrow. Come go in,
I'll show thee some attires, and have thy counsel
Which is the best to furnish me to-morrow.

Ursula   [*Aside.*] She's limed, I warrant you. We
have caught her, madam.

Hero   [*Aside.*] If it proves so, then loving goes
105   by haps:
Some Cupid kills with arrows, some with traps.

                                   [*Exeunt Hero and Ursula.*]

Beatrice   [*Coming forward.*] What fire is in mine ears?
        Can this be true?
Stand I condemn'd for pride and scorn so much?
Contempt, farewell, and maiden pride, adieu!
110   No glory lives behind the back of such.
And, Benedick, love on, I will requite thee,
Taming my wild heart to thy loving hand.
If thou dost love, my kindness shall incite thee
To bind our loves up in a holy band;
115   For others say thou dost deserve, and I
Believe it better than reportingly.

                                              Exit.

Scene 2

Enter Prince [**Don Pedro**], **Claudio**, **Benedick**, *and*
Leonato.

Don Pedro   I do but stay till your marriage be
consummate, and then go I toward Arragon.

Claudio   I'll bring you thither, my lord, if you'll
4   vouchsafe me.

Hero   Why, after tomorrow, I will be married every day. Come, let's go in. I want to get your advice on which would be the best clothes to wear tomorrow.

Ursula   [*aside to Hero*] I swear, she's trapped; we caught her, madam.

Hero   [*aside to Ursula*] If that is true, then love happens by chance. Cupid catches some with arrows and others he catches with traps.

[*Hero and Ursula exit.*]

Beatrice   [*moving forward*] My ears are burning. Is this true? Have I been criticized this much for my pride and scorn? Well, good-bye contempt! Adieu maiden pride! There is no glory in standing behind such traits. And as for Benedick, love on. I will return your love and tame my wild heart to your loving hand. If you do love me, my kindness will cause you to bind our love in marriage. They say that you are deserving of my love and I believe it, and not just because they say so.

[*Beatrice exits.*]

Scene 2

Enter **Don Pedro, Claudio, Benedick,** *and* **Leonato** *in a room in Leonato's house.*

Don Pedro   I'm going to stay until your wedding is over and then I will go to Aragon.

Claudio   I'll escort you to Aragon, my lord, if you'll let me.

121

Don Pedro   Nay, that would be as great a soil
in the new gloss of your marriage as to show a child
his new coat and forbid him to wear it. I will only
be bold with Benedick for his company, for from
the crown of his head to the sole of his foot, he is all
10   mirth. He hath twice or thrice cut Cupid's
bow-string, and the little hangman dare not shoot
at him. He hath a heart as sound as a bell, and his
tongue is the clapper, for what his heart thinks, his
tongue speaks.

15 **Benedick**   Gallants, I am not as I have been.

Leonato   So say I, methinks you are sadder.

Claudio   I hope he be in love.

Don Pedro   Hang him, truant, there's no true
drop of blood in him to be truly touch'd with love.
20   If he be sad, he wants money.

Benedick   I have the toothache.

Don Pedro   Draw it.

Benedick   Hang it!

Claudio   You must hang it first, and draw it after-
25   wards.

Don Pedro   What? sigh for the toothache?

Leonato   Where is but a humor or a worm.

Benedick   Well, every one [can] master a grief but
he that has it.

30 **Claudio**   Yet say I, he is in love.

Don Pedro   No, that would be as huge a blemish on your new marriage as it would be to show a child his new coat and not allow him to wear it. I will take the liberty of asking Benedick to accompany me, because from the top of his head to the soles of his feet, he is a comedian. He has managed to escape Cupid's arrow two or three times now, and the little torturer is afraid to shoot at him. Benedick's heart is like the sound of a bell with his tongue as the clapper, because whatever his heart feels, his tongue speaks.

Benedick   Gentlemen, I am not my old self.

Leonato   So you say. I think you are more serious.

Claudio   I hope he is in love.

Don Pedro   Darn it man! There is no possible way that Benedick could ever be truly in love; if he is serious, he wants money.

Benedick   I have a toothache.

Don Pedro   Well, pull it out.

Benedick   Darn!

Claudio   You must hang it first, and pull it afterwards.

Don Pedro   What! Is that sigh for the toothache?

Leonato   It is obviously caused by a foul secretion or a tooth worm.

Benedick   Well, everyone is able to heal from suffering except for the person who is suffering.

Claudio   I still think he is in love.

Don Pedro   There is no appearance of fancy in
him, unless it be a fancy that he hath to strange
disguises—as to be a Dutchman to-day, a Frenchman to-morrow, or in the shape of two countries
at once, as a German from the waist downward,
36   all slops, and a Spaniard from the hip upward,
no doublet. Unless he have a fancy to this foolery,
as it appears he hath, he is no fool for fancy, as you
39   would have it appear he is.

Claudio   If he be not in love with some woman,
there is no believing old signs. 'A brushes his hat
a' mornings; what should that bode?

Don Pedro   Hath any man seen him at the barber's?

45 **Claudio**   No, but the barber's man hath been
seen with him, and the old ornament of his cheek hath
already stuff'd tennis-balls.

Leonato   Indeed he looks younger than he did, by
the loss of a beard.

Don Pedro   Nay, 'a rubs himself with civet. Can
51   you smell him out by that?

Claudio   That's as much as to say, the sweet youth's
in love.

Don Pedro   The greatest note of it is his melan-
55   choly.

Claudio   And when was he wont to wash his face?

Don Pedro   Yea, or to paint himself? for the which
I hear what they say of him.

Claudio   Nay, but his jesting spirit, which is now
crept into a lute-string, and now govern'd by stops.

Don Pedro   There is no sign of love in him, unless Benedick is trying to strangely disguise love as a Dutchman today and a Frenchman tomorrow or as two countries at one time: a German from the waist down with baggy pants and socks, and a Spaniard from the waist up, without a vest. Perhaps he has a love for foolishness, which is what it seems, because he is not a fool for love as you think he is.

Claudio   If he is not in love with some woman then you can't believe in the usual symptoms. He brushes his hat in the morning, what does that mean?

Don Pedro   Has anyone seen him at the barber's?

Claudio   No, but the barber's helper has been seen with Benedick. Benedick's beard is now being used to stuff tennis balls.

Leonato   Yes, he looks younger without his beard.

Don Pedro   So he wears cologne; can you find out his secret with that?

Claudio   That's proof enough that the sweet smelling young man is in love.

Don Pedro   The most noticeable sign is his seriousness.

Claudio   And when has he ever wanted to wash his face?

Don Pedro   Yes, or to use cosmetics? And I've heard what they are saying about him for using cosmetics.

Claudio   In fact, his sarcastic spirit seems to have turned into lute strings which can be silenced just like the stops on the instrument.

Don Pedro   Indeed that tells a heavy tale for him.
62   Conclude, conclude, he is in love.

Claudio   Nay, but I know who loves him.

Don Pedro   That would I know too. I warrant
65   one that knows him not.

Claudio   Yes, and his ill conditions, and in despite
of all, dies for him.

Don Pedro   She shall be buried with her face up-
69   wards.

Benedick   Yet is this no charm for the toothache.
Old signior, walk aside with me, I have studied
eight or nine wise words to speak to you, which
these hobby-horses must not hear.

[*Exeunt Benedick and Leonato.*]

Don Pedro   For my life, to break with him about
75   Beatrice.

Claudio   'Tis even so. Hero and Margaret have
by this play'd their parts with Beatrice, and then
the two bears will not bite one another when they
79   meet.

Enter [**Don**] **John** *the Bastard.*

Don John   My lord and brother, God save you!

Don Pedro   Good den, brother.

Don John   If your leisure serv'd, I would speak
with you.

84   **Don Pedro**   In private?

Don John   If it please you, yet Count Claudio may
hear, for what I would speak of concerns him.

Don Pedro   Truly, this all tells a serious tale for him, concluding that he is in love.

Claudio   Indeed, and I know who loves him.

Don Pedro   I know too: someone who obviously doesn't know him at all.

Claudio   Yes, and despite knowing all of his bad qualities, she "dies" for him.

Don Pedro   She'll be buried with her face up.

Benedick   This is certainly no cure for a toothache. Old Signior, walk with me; I have eight or nine well-chosen words I'd like to say to you and I don't want these buffoons to hear.

[*Benedick and Leonato exit.*]

Don Pedro   Upon my life, he is going to speak with him about Beatrice.

Claudio   It's true. By now, Hero and Margaret have played their roles with Beatrice and now these two bears will not bite each other when they meet.

[*Enter* **Don John.**]

Don John   My lord and brother, God save you!

Don Pedro   Good evening, brother.

Don John   If you have time, I would like to speak with you.

Don Pedro   In private?

Don John   If that's what you'd like, but what I have to say concerns Count Claudio and he may want to hear it.

Don Pedro   What's the matter?

Don John   [*To Claudio.*] Means your lordship to be married
to-morrow?

90 **Don Pedro**   You know he does.

Don John   I know not that, when he knows what
I know.

Claudio   If there be any impediment, I pray you
94   discover it.

Don John   You may think I love you not; let that
appear hereafter, and aim better at me by that I
now will manifest. For my brother, I think he holds
you well, and in dearness of heart hath holp to effect
your ensuing marriage—surely suit ill spent and
100   labor ill bestow'd.

Don Pedro   Why, what's the matter?

Don John   I came hither to tell you, and circum-
stances short'ned (for she has been too long a-talking
of), the lady is disloyal.

105 **Claudio**   Who, Hero?

Don John   Even she—Leonato's Hero, your Hero,
every man's Hero.

Claudio   Disloyal?

Don John   The word is too good to paint out her
110   wickedness. I could say she were worse; think
you of a worse title, and I will fit her to it. Wonder not
till further warrant. Go but with me to-night, you
shall see her chamber-window ent'red, even the night
before her wedding-day. If you love her then,
to-morrow wed her; but it would better fit your
116   honor to change your mind.

Don Pedro   What's the matter?

Don John   [*to Claudio*] Are you going to be married tomorrow?

Don Pedro   You know he is.

Don John   When he knows what I know, I really won't know that.

Claudio   If there is any reason to prevent it, please tell me.

Don John   You may think that I don't love you, but hopefully after you hear what I have to say, you will think better of me. My brother thinks highly of you and has helped arrange your upcoming marriage, which was a waste of time and energy.

Don Pedro   Why, what's the matter?

Don John   I've come to tell you. She's not worth the time we've already spent talking about her so I'll make this short: The woman is unfaithful.

Claudio   Who, Hero?

Don John   Yes, her. Leonato's Hero, your Hero, everyone's Hero.

Claudio   Unfaithful?

Don John   The word is too good to describe her wickedness; I can think of something worse to call her, as could you, and it would fit her. You won't question it when you see proof. Go with me tonight and you will see someone enter her bedroom window, and this, the night before her wedding. If you still love her after that, marry her tomorrow, but it would be best for your honorable reputation if you changed your mind.

Claudio   May this be so?

Don Pedro   I will not think it.

Don John   If you dare not trust that you see,
120   confess not that you know. If you will follow me,
I will show you enough, and when you have seen
more, and heard more, proceed accordingly.

Claudio   If I see any thing to-night why I should
not marry her, to-morrow in the congregation,
125   where I should wed, there will I shame her.

Don Pedro   And as I woo'd for thee to obtain her,
I will join with thee to disgrace her.

Don John   I will disparage her no farther till you
are my witnesses. Bear it coldly but till midnight,
130   and let the issue show itself.

Don Pedro   O day untowardly turn'd!

Claudio   O mischief strangely thwarting!

Don John   O plague right well prevented! So will
you say when you have seen the sequel.

                                                  [Exeunt.]

Scene 3

Enter **Dogberry** *and his compartner* [**Verges**] *with the* **Watch**.

Dogberry   Are you good men and true?

Verges   Yea, or else it were pity but they should
suffer salvation, body and soul.

Claudio   Can this be true?

Don Pedro   I can't imagine it.

Don John   If you don't trust what you see, then don't say that you know what she's like. If you follow me, I'll show you enough and once you have seen more and heard more, then make a decision.

Claudio   If I see any reason tonight why I shouldn't marry her tomorrow, I will disgrace her in front of the very congregation where I would have married her.

Don Pedro   And, because I encouraged you to pursue her in marriage, I will support you in disgracing her.

Don John   I won't belittle her any further until you see proof yourselves. Be calm and wait until midnight, and the problem will reveal itself.

Don Pedro   Oh, this day has turned into a disaster!

Claudio   Oh, and it is strangely threatened by mischief!

Don John   Oh, and a calamity prevented! Or that's what you'll say when you have seen how this plays out.

[*They all exit.*]

Scene 3

Enter **Dogberry** *and* **Verges** *with the* **Watch** *on a street.*

Dogberry   Are you trustworthy and loyal men?

Verges   Yes, or else it would be a shame if they should suffer salvation [*he means "damnation"*] body and soul.

Dogberry   Nay, that were a punishment too good for
them, if they should have any allegiance in them,
6   being chosen for the Prince's watch.

Verges   Well, give them their charge, neighbor
Dogberry.

Dogberry   First, who think you the most desartless
10   man to be constable?

1st Watchman   Hugh Oatcake, sir, or George Seacole,
for they can write and read.

Dogberry   Come hither, neighbor Seacole. God hath
blest you with a good name. To be a well-favor'd
man is the gift of fortune, but to write and read comes
16   by nature.

2nd Watchman   Both which, Master Constable—

Dogberry   You have: I knew it would be your answer.
Well, for your favor, sir, why, give God thanks,
20   and make no boast of it, and for your writing
and reading, let that appear when there is no need of
such vanity. You are thought here to be the most
senseless and fit man for the constable of the watch;
therefore bear you the lanthorn. This is your charge:
you shall comprehend all vagrom men; you are to
26   bid any man stand, in the Prince's name.

2nd Watchman   How if 'a will not stand?

Dogberry   Why then take no note of him, but let him
go, and presently call the rest of the watch together,
30   and thank God you are rid of a knave.

Verges   If he will not stand when he is bidden, he
is none of the Prince's subjects.

Dogberry   Indeed, that punishment would be too good for them, if they had any allegiance [*he means "disloyalty"*], being chosen for the Prince's watch.

Verges   Well, give them their charge, neighbor Dogberry.

Dogberry   First, who do you think is the most desertless [*he means "deserving"*] man to be head watchman?

First Watchman   Either Hugh Otecake, sir, or George Seacoal because they can write and read.

Dogberry   Come here, neighbor Seacoal. God has blessed you with a good name, and to be good-looking is a gift of luck, but to write and read comes naturally.

Second Watchman   Both of them or which, master constable?

Dogberry   You have, I knew that would be your answer. Well, give God thanks for your looks and don't brag about it. As for your writing and reading, use it only when you can't use your looks. You are thought to be the most sense-less [*he means "sensible"*] and fit man to be the head of the watch and you will carry the lantern. This is your assignment: You shall comprehend [*he means "apprehend"*] all vagrom [*he means "vagrant"*] men; you are to ask them to stop in the name of the Prince.

Second Watchman   What if he won't stop?

Dogberry   Why, then, don't pay any attention to him and let him go. And then call the rest of the watch together and thank God that you have gotten rid of the villain.

Verges   If he will not stop when he is asked, then he is not one of the Prince's subjects.

Dogberry   True, and they are to meddle with none
but the Prince's subjects. You shall also make no
35   noise in the streets; for, for the watch to babble
and to talk, is most tolerable, and not to be endur'd.

2nd Watchman   We will rather sleep than talk, we
know what belongs to a watch.

Dogberry   Why, you speak like an ancient and most
40   quiet watchman, for I cannot see how sleeping
should offend; only have a care that your bills be not
stol'n. Well, you are to call at all the alehouses, and
bid those that are drunk get them to bed.

2nd Watchman   How if they will not?

Dogberry   Why then let them alone till they are
46   sober. If they make you not then the better
answer, you may say they are not the men you took
them for.

2nd Watchman   Well, sir.

Dogberry   If you meet a thief, you may suspect him,
51   by virtue of your office, to be no true man; and
for such kind of men, the less you meddle or make
with them, why, the more is for your honesty.

2nd Watchman   If we know him to be a thief, shall
55   we not lay hands on him?

Dogberry   Truly by your office you may, but I think
they that touch pitch will be defil'd. The most peaceable way for you, if you do take a thief, is to let him
show himself what he is, and steal out of your com-
60   pany.

Verges   You have been always call'd a merciful
man, partner.

Dogberry   True. And they shouldn't interfere with any of the Prince's subjects. Don't make any noise in the streets. To have the watchmen jabber and talk is most tolerable [*he means "intolerable"*] and will not be tolerated.

Second Watchman   We would rather sleep than talk; we know what is appropriate for watchmen.

Dogberry   You speak like an experienced and quiet watchman; I don't think that sleeping should be a problem, but be careful so that your weapons aren't stolen. Remember to visit all of the alehouses and tell all those who are drunk to get to bed.

Second Watchman   And what if they won't?

Dogberry   Well, then, leave them alone until they are sober and if they still don't listen, tell them that they aren't the men you were looking for after all.

Second Watchman   Okay, sir.

Dogberry   If you meet a thief, then you already know him to be a dishonest man, because that's the kind of men they are and the less you interfere or have to do with them, the more honest you are.

Second Watchman   If we know that he is a thief, shouldn't we arrest him?

Dogberry   Yes, as a watchman you could, but I think that those who touch something dirty will get dirty. The most peaceable thing to do if you catch a thief is to let him show you who he really is and steal his way out of your presence.

Verges   You have always been known as a merciful man, partner.

Dogberry   Truly, I would not hang a dog by my will,
much more a man who hath any honesty in him.

Verges   If you hear a child cry in the night, you
66   must call to the nurse and bid her still it.

2nd Watchman   How if the nurse be asleep and will
not hear us?

Dogberry   Why then depart in peace, and let the
child wake her with crying, for the ewe that will not
hear her lamb when it baes will never answer a calf
72   when he bleats.

Verges   'Tis very true.

Dogberry   This is the end of the charge: you, constable,
are to present the Prince's own person. If you meet
76   the Prince in the night, you may stay him.

Verges   Nay, by'r our lady, that I think 'a cannot.

Dogberry   Five shillings to one on't, with any man
that knows the [statues], he may stay him; marry,
not without the Prince be willing, for indeed the
watch ought to offend no man, and it is an offense to
82   stay a man against his will.

Verges   By'r lady, I think it be so.

Dogberry   Ha, ah ha! Well, masters, good night.
And there be any matter of weight chances, call up
me. Keep your fellows' counsels and your own, and
87   good night. Come, neighbor.

2nd Watchman   Well, masters, we hear our charge.
Let us go sit here upon the church-bench till two, and
90   then all to bed.

Dogberry   Yes, I wouldn't hang a dog much more [*he means "much less"*] a man who is in the least bit honest.

Verges   If you hear a child cry in the night, you must call to the nurse and ask her to calm it.

Second Watchman   What if the nurse is asleep and doesn't hear us?

Dogberry   Well then, depart in peace and let the child's crying wake her. For the ewe that doesn't hear her own lamb when it baas will never answer a calf when it bleats.

Verges   This is very true.

Dogberry   This is the end of the assignment. You watchmen are representing the Prince: If you meet the Prince during the night you can ask him to stop.

Verges   Truthfully, by an oath of our Lady [referring to Mother Mary], I don't think you can.

Dogberry   I'll bet five shillings to one on it with any man who knows the laws. He may stop him, however, not without the Prince's permission. Because, of course, the watch shouldn't offend any man, and it is an offense to keep a man against his will.

Verges   By an oath of our Lady, I think that's true.

Dogberry   Ha, ha, ha! Well, masters, good night. If anything important happens, call me. Keep each other's secrets as well as your own. Good night. Come, neighbor.

Second Watchman   Well, masters, we've heard our assignment, let's sit here on the church bench until two, and then we'll go to bed.

Dogberry   One word more, honest neighbors. I pray
you watch about Signior Leonato's door, for the
wedding being there to-morrow, there is a great
coil to-night. Adieu! Be vigitant, I beseech you.

Exeunt [*Dogberry and Verges*].

Enter **Borachio** *and* **Conrade**.

95 **Borachio**   What, Conrade!

2nd Watchman   [*Aside.*] Peace, stir not.

Borachio   Conrade, I say!

Conrade   Here, man, I am at thy elbow.

Borachio   Mass, and my elbow itch'd; I thought there
100   would a scab follow.

Conrade   I will owe thee an answer for that, and now
forward with thy tale.

Borachio   Stand thee close then under this penthouse,
for it drizzles rain, and I will, like a true drunkard,
105   utter all to thee.

2nd Watchman   [*Aside.*] Some treason, masters, yet
stand close.

Borachio   Therefore know I have earn'd of Don John
a thousand ducats.

Conrade   Is it possible that any villany should be
111   so dear?

Borachio   Thou shouldst rather ask if it were possible
any villany should be so rich; for when rich villains
have need of poor ones, poor ones may make what
115   price they will.

Conrade   I wonder at it.

Dogberry   One more thing, honest neighbors. Please keep a watch around Signior Leonato's house. Because of the wedding being held there tomorrow there is a lot of commotion around there tonight. Adieu. I beg you, be vigitant [*he means "vigilant"*].

[*Dogberry and Verges exit.*]

[**Borachio** *and* **Conrade** *enter.*]

Borachio   Conrade!

Second Watchman   [*Aside*] Peace! Be quiet.

Borachio   I say, Conrade!

Conrade   Here, man; I'm right here at your elbow.

Borachio   I swear, I thought my elbow was itching because I had a scab there.

Conrade   I will get you back for that answer, but for now, tell me your story.

Borachio   Stay here under this overhang out of the rain and, like a true drunk, I'll tell you the whole story.

Second Watchman   [*Aside*] Some treachery, masters. Stay here.

Borachio   You should know that I have earned a thousand gold coins from Don John because of it.

Conrade   Is it possible that such wickedness should be so valuable?

Borachio   Instead you should ask if it is possible for any villain to be so rich. Because when rich villains need poor villains, the poor ones can ask whatever price they want.

Conrade   I am truly amazed.

Borachio   That shows thou art unconfirm'd. Thou
knowest that the fashion of a doublet, or a hat, or a
cloak, is nothing to a man.

120 **Conrade**   Yes, it is apparel.

Borachio   I mean the fashion.

Conrade   Yes, the fashion is the fashion.

Borachio   Tush, I may as well say the fool's the fool.
But seest thou not what a deformed thief this fashion is?

2nd Watchman   [*Aside.*] I know that Deformed; 'a
has been a vile thief this seven year; 'a goes up and
127   down like a gentleman. I remember his name.

Borachio   Didst thou not hear somebody?

Conrade   No, 'twas the vane on the house.

Borachio   Seest thou not, I say, what a deformed
thief this fashion is, how giddily 'a turns about all
132   the hot bloods between fourteen and five-and-
thirty, sometimes fashioning them like Pharaoh's
soldiers in the reechy painting, sometime like god
Bel's priests in the old church-window, sometime
like the shaven Hercules in the smirch'd worm-eaten
tapestry, where his codpiece seems as massy as
138   his club?

Conrade   All this I see, and I see that the fashion
wears out more apparel than the man. But art not
thou thyself giddy with the fashion too, that thou
hast shifted out of thy tale into telling me of the
143   fashion?

Borachio   That shows that you are uninformed. You know that the style of a vest, a hat, or a coat means nothing to a man.

Conrade   Yes, because it's just clothing.

Borachio   I mean, the fashion [style] of a man's clothing tells you nothing about the man.

Conrade   Yes, because the fashion is the fashion.

Borachio   Please! I might as well say the fool's the fool. But don't you see how this constantly changing fashion is a deformed thief that robs a man of his money?

Second Watchman   [*aside*] I know that this "Deformed" has been a despicable thief these past seven years, going here and there like a gentleman. I remember his name.

Borachio   Didn't you hear anyone?

Conrade   No, it was the weather vane moving on the house.

Borachio   Don't you understand what I am saying about what a deformed thief that fashion is and how happily it changes all of the hot-blooded men between fourteen and fifty-three? How it changes them into the Pharaoh's soldiers in a smoky painting and sometimes like the priests of Baal in the church's stained-glass windows and sometimes like a shaved Hercules in the filthy and worm-eaten tapestry where his codpiece is as big as his club?

Conrade   Yes, I understand that fashion wears out more clothes than a man does. But aren't you just as excited about fashion to have changed the subject from telling me your story into telling me about fashion?

Borachio   Not so neither, but know that I have
to-night woo'd Margaret, the Lady Hero's gentlewoman, by the name of Hero. She leans me out at her
147   mistress' chamber-window, bids me a thousand
times good night—I tell this tale vildly, I should first
tell thee how the Prince, Claudio, and my master,
planted and plac'd and possess'd by my master Don
John, saw afar off in the orchard this amiable en-
152   counter.

Conrade   And thought they Margaret was Hero?

Borachio   Two of them did, the Prince and Claudio,
but the devil my master knew she was Margaret; and
partly by his oaths, which first possess'd them, partly
157   by the dark night, which did deceive them, but
chiefly by my villainy, which did confirm any slander
that Don John had made, away went Claudio enrag'd;
swore he would meet her as he was appointed next
morning at the temple, and there, before the whole
162   congregation, shame her with what he saw o'er-
night, and send her home again without a husband.

2nd Watchman   We charge you, in the Prince's name,
stand!

1st Watchman   Call up the right Master Constable.
167   We have here recover'd the most dangerous piece
of lechery that ever was known in the commonwealth.

2nd Watchman   And one Deformed is one of them; I
know him, 'a wears a lock.

171 **Conrade**   Masters, masters—

2nd Watchman   You'll be made bring Deformed forth,
I warrant you.

Conrade   Masters—

Borachio   That is not so, but you need to know that tonight I seduced Lady Hero's gentlewoman, Margaret. I called her "Hero" as she leaned me out of her mistress's bedroom window and said good night to me a thousand times. I'm telling this awkwardly. I should first tell you that my master Don John arranged for the Prince and Claudio to be in the nearby orchard to witness the romantic encounter.

Conrade   And they thought Margaret was Hero?

Borachio   The Prince and Claudio did, but my master, the devil knew she was Margaret. They believed it partially because of the story Don John told them earlier and partially because the dark night is deceiving, but mostly because of my treachery, which confirmed the lies that Don John had made up. Claudio went away so enraged that he swore he would meet her at the temple at the appointed time the next morning and in front of the entire congregation, he would disgrace her with what he had seen the night before and send her home without a husband.

Second Watchman   We charge you, in the Prince's name, stop!

First Watchman   Call the master constable. We have recovered [*he means "discovered"*] the most dangerous piece of lechery [*he means "treachery"*] that has ever been seen in the commonwealth.

Second Watchman   And one who is named Deformed is one of them. I know him because he wears his hair long.

Conrade   Gentlemen, gentlemen.

Second Watchman   I swear, you will be forced to bring Deformed forth.

Conrade   Gentlemen—

143

2nd Watchman   Never speak, we charge you; let us
176   obey you to go with us.

Borachio   We are like to prove a goodly commodity,
being taken up of these men's bills.

Conrade   A commodity in question, I warrant you.
Come, we'll obey you.

[*Exeunt.*]

Scene 4

Enter **Hero** *and* **Margaret** *and* **Ursula**.

Hero   Good Ursula, wake my cousin Beatrice,
and desire her to rise.

Ursula   I will, lady.

Hero   And bid her come hither.

5 **Ursula**   Well.

[*Exit.*]

Margaret   Troth, I think your other rabato were
better.

Hero   No, pray thee, good Meg, I'll wear this.

Margaret   By my troth 's not so good, and I warrant
10   your cousin will say so.

Hero   My cousin's a fool, and thou art another.
I'll wear none but this.

Second Watchman   Don't speak. We demand that you let us obey you [*he means "obey us"*] and go with us.

Borachio   We are probably a valuable piece of merchandise being taken by these men's weapons.

Conrade   Well, the value of the merchandise is questionable I promise you. Come, we will obey you.

[*They all exit.*]

Scene 4

Enter **Hero**, **Margaret**, *and* **Ursula** *in Hero's bedroom.*

Hero   Good Ursula, wake Beatrice and ask her to get up.

Ursula   I will, lady.

Hero   And then ask her to come here.

Ursula   Will do.

[*Ursula exits.*]

Margaret   Truthfully, I think your other collar is a better choice.

Hero   No, please, Meg, I'll wear this one.

Margaret   Truthfully, it's not a good choice and I know your cousin will agree.

Hero   My cousin's a fool and so are you. I'm not going to wear any of them except this.

Margaret   I like the new tire within excellently, if
the hair were a thought browner; and your gown's
a most rare fashion, i' faith. I saw the Duchess of
16 Milan's gown that they praise so.

Hero   O, that exceeds, they say.

Margaret   By my troth 's but a night-gown [in] respect of yours: cloth a' gold and cuts, and lac'd
20 with silver, set with pearls, down sleeves, side
sleeves, and skirts, round underborne with a bluish
tinsel; but for a fine, quaint, graceful, and excellent
fashion, yours is worth ten on't.

Hero   God give me joy to wear it, for my heart is
25 exceeding heavy.

Margaret   'Twill be heavier soon by the weight of a
man.

Hero   Fie upon thee, art not asham'd?

Margaret   Of what, lady? of speaking honorably?
30 Is not marriage honorable in a beggar? Is not
your lord honourable without marriage? I think
you would have me say, "saving your reverence, a
husband." And bad thinking do not wrest true
speaking, I'll offend nobody. Is there any harm
35 in "the heavier for a husband"? None, I think,
and it be the right husband and the right wife; otherwise 'tis light, and not heavy. Ask my Lady Beatrice
else, here she comes.

Enter **Beatrice**.

Hero   Good morrow, coz.

40 **Beatrice**   Good morrow, sweet Hero.

Margaret I like the new headdress here very much, if only the hairpiece were a bit darker. Your dress is unusually fashionable. Honest, I saw the Duchess of Milan's gown that everyone loves so much.

Hero Oh, they say it is wonderful.

Margaret Honestly it is, but it looks like a nightgown in comparison to yours. The cloth it is made of has gold threads with cut-outs, and it is laced with silver and pearls, with long, narrow sleeves and ornamental side sleeves. The skirts are trimmed along the hem with a bluish metallic cloth. But considering such a superior, appealing, elegant, and outstanding piece of fashion, your dress is worth ten of them.

Hero I hope that I will enjoy wearing it, because my heart is extremely heavy.

Margaret It'll be even heavier with the weight of a man.

Hero Oh, you! You should be ashamed of yourself!

Margaret Ashamed of what, lady? For speaking honestly? Isn't marriage respectable even for a beggar? Isn't your lord respectable without marriage? I think that you would prefer I say, excuse me for saying this, a husband. If vulgar thoughts do not distort the truth, I won't offend anyone. Is there anything wrong in saying you'll be heavier because of a husband? No, I don't think so as long as it is the right husband and the right wife, otherwise it would be immoral and not heavy. Ask Lady Beatrice if this is true, here she comes.

[**Beatrice** *enters.*]

Hero Good morning, cousin.

Beatrice Good morning, sweet Hero.

Hero   Why, how now? Do you speak in the
sick tune?

Beatrice   I am out of all other tune, methinks.

Margaret   Clap 's into "Light a' love"; that goes
without a burden. Do you sing it, and I'll dance
46   it.

Beatrice   Ye light a' love with your heels! then if
your husband have stables enough, you'll see he shall
lack no barns.

Margaret   O illegitimate construction! I scorn that
51   with my heels.

Beatrice   'Tis almost five a'clock, cousin, 'tis time
you were ready. By my troth, I am exceeding ill.
Heigh-ho!

55 **Margaret**   For a hawk, a horse, or a husband?

Beatrice   For the letter that begins them all, H.

Margaret   Well, and you be not turn'd Turk, there's
no more sailing by the star.

Beatrice   What means the fool, trow?

Margaret   Nothing I, but God send every one their
61   heart's desire!

Hero   These gloves the Count sent me, they are
an excellent perfume.

Beatrice   I am stuff'd, cousin; I cannot smell.

Margaret   A maid, and stuff'd! There's goodly
66   catching of cold.

Hero   What's wrong, you sound like you are sick?

Beatrice   I'm afraid that's the only tune I am capable of right now.

Margaret   Let's swing into "Light o' Love." It is an easy song, and if you sing it, I'll dance to it.

Beatrice   You are shameless and unchaste! And if your wealthy husband has enough rooms, you'll not lack the children to fill them.

Margaret   Oh, that's completely wrong, and I reject that kind of life contemptuously.

Beatrice   It's almost five o'clock, cousin, and you should be ready. Honestly, I feel really sick, ho-hum.

Margaret   Are you sick for a hawk, a horse, or a husband?

Beatrice   I am sick with an "H" ["*ache*" *was pronounced "aich" like the sound of the letter "H"*], the letter that begins all of them.

Margaret   Well, if you haven't abandoned your old faith, then you really can't trust being guided by the North Star any longer.

Beatrice   I wonder what the fool means?

Margaret   I don't mean anything, but God does give everyone what their heart truly wishes for!

Hero   The scented gloves that the count sent to me smell beautifully.

Beatrice   Cousin, I am all stuffed up and can't smell anything.

Margaret   A virgin and pregnant! That's a good way to catch a cold.

Beatrice   O, God help me, God help me, how long
have you profess'd apprehension?

Margaret   Even since you left it. Doth not my wit
70   become me rarely?

Beatrice   It is not seen enough, you should wear it
in your cap. By my troth, I am sick.

Margaret   Get you some of this distill'd *carduus
benedictus*, and lay it to your heart; it is the only
75   thing for a qualm.

Hero   There thou prick'st her with a thistle.

Beatrice   *Benedictus*! why *benedictus*? You have
some moral in this *benedictus*.

Margaret   Moral? no, by my troth, I have no mor-
80   al meaning, I meant plain holy-thistle. You
may think perchance that I think you are in love.
Nay, by'r lady, I am not such a fool to think what
I list, nor I list not to think what I can, nor indeed
I cannot think, if I would think my heart out of
85   thinking, that you are in love, or that you will be
in love, or that you can be in love. Yet Benedick
was such another, and now is he become a man.
He swore he would never marry, and yet now in
despite of his heart he eats his meat without grudg-
90   ing; and how you may be converted I know
not, but methinks you look with your eyes as other
women do.

Beatrice   What pace is this that thy tongue keeps?

94 **Margaret**   Not a false gallop.

Beatrice   Oh, God please help me! God help me! How long has wittiness been your profession?

Margaret   Ever since you left yours behind. Wit suits me well, doesn't it?

Beatrice   It is not seen often enough—you should wear it in your cap like a fool wears his coxcomb. Seriously, I am sick.

Margaret   Get some "Carduus Benedictus" [*a pun on the word carduus, which means "blessed thistle," and the name "Benedick"*] and put it on your heart. It's the only thing that will cure a sudden illness.

Hero   There, now you've really pricked her with a thistle.

Beatrice   Benedictus! Why Benedictus? Do you have some hidden meaning in the word "Benedictus"?

Margaret   Hidden meaning! Of course not, I have no hidden meaning. I simply meant holy-thistle. You might think that I think you are in love, but by Our Lady, I am not foolish enough to think what I choose, nor can I choose not to think what I can, nor can I not think, if I convince myself out of thinking, that you are in love or that you will be in love or that you can be in love. Benedick is another person who swore that he would never marry and now, despite his true self, is content to be like other men and marry. Now, how you are going to be changed I do not know, but I think that you too are beginning to see the way other women do.

Beatrice   How can you talk at such a pace?

Margaret   Well, at least it's not untrue banter.

Enter **Ursula**.

Ursula   Madam, withdraw, the Prince, the Count, Signior
Benedick, Don John, and all the gallants of the town are
come to fetch you to church.

Hero   Help to dress me, good coz, good Meg, good Ursula.

[*Exeunt.*]

Scene 5

Enter **Leonato** *and the Constable* [**Dogberry**] *and the*
Headborough [**Verges**].

Leonato   What would you with me, honest neighbor?

Dogberry   Marry, sir, I would have some confidence
with you that decerns you nearly.

Leonato   Brief, I pray you, for you see it is a busy
5   time with me.

Dogberry   Marry, this it is, sir.

Verges   Yes, in truth it is, sir.

Leonato   What is it, my good friends?

Dogberry   Goodman Verges, sir, speaks a little [off] the
matter; an old man, sir, and his wits are not so blunt
as, God help, I would desire they were, but in faith,
12   honest as the skin between his brows.

Verges   Yes, I thank God I am as honest as any
man living, that is an old man, and no honester
than I.

[**Ursula** *re-enters.*]

Ursula   Madam, let's leave. The Prince, the count, Signior Benedick, Don John, and all the fashionable young men of the town have come to bring you to church.

Hero   Help me get dressed, good cousin, good Meg, good Ursula.

[*They all exit.*]

Scene 5

*Enter **Leonato**, with **Dogberry** and **Verges**, in another room in the house.*

Leonato   What would you like from me, good neighbor?

Dogberry   Indeed, sir, I would like to speak with you about something that dearly decerns [*he means "concerns"*] you.

Leonato   Be quick please, you can see that I am really busy.

Dogberry   Indeed, this is it, sir.

Verges   Yes, it is the truth, sir.

Leonato   What is it, my good friends?

Dogberry   Good man Verges here speaks a little off the subject, sir. He's an old man and his wits are not as blunt [*he means "sharp"*] as I would like, God help me, but in truth, he is as honest as the skin between his brows.

Verges   Yes, thank God I am as honest as any old man, and no one is more honest than me.

Dogberry   Comparisons are odorous—*palabras*, neigh-
17   bor Verges.

Leonato   Neighbors, you are tedious.

Dogberry   It pleases your worship to say so, but we
are the poor Duke's officers; but truly, for mine own
part, if I were as tedious as a king, I could find in
22   my heart to bestow it all of your worship.

Leonato   All thy tediousness on me, ah?

Dogberry   Yea, and 'twere a thousand pound more
than 'tis, for I hear as good exclamation on your
worship as of any man in the city, and though I be
27   but a poor man, I am glad to hear it.

Verges   And so am I.

Leonato   I would fain know what you have to say.

Verges   Marry, sir, our watch to-night, excepting
your worship's presence, ha' ta'en a couple of as
arrant knaves as any in Messina.

Dogberry   A good old man, sir, he will be talking;
34   as they say, "When the age is in, the wit is out."
God help us, it is a world to see! Well said, i' faith,
neighbor Verges. Well, God's a good man; and
two men ride of a horse, one must ride behind.
An honest soul, i' faith, sir, by my troth he is, as
ever broke bread; but God is to be worshipp'd; all
40   men are not alike, alas, good neighbor!

Leonato   Indeed, neighbor, he comes too short of
you.

Dogberry   Gifts that God gives.

44 **Leonato**   I must leave you.

Dogberry Comparisons are odorous [*he means "odious" or "detestable"*]; use few words, neighbor Verges.

Leonato Neighbors, you are tedious.

Dogberry Thank you for saying so, but we are only the poor duke's officers. And honestly, for me, if I were as tedious [*he means "wealthy"*] as a king, I would give it all to you, your worship.

Leonato You would give all your tediousness to me, ah?

Dogberry Yes, and if I could give a thousand pounds more than that I would because I hear as good an exclamation [*he means "acclaim"*] about you as any man in the city, and even though I am a poor man, I am happy to hear it.

Verges And so am I.

Leonato I would really like to know what you want to say.

Verges Indeed sir, last night our watchmen, excepting [*he means "respecting"*] your presence, arrested two of the worst criminals ever seen in Messina.

Dogberry He's a good old man, sir, though he babbles on; as they say, when you get older, you lose your wit. God help us! It is an amazing world. Well said, honestly, neighbor Verges. Well, God's a fair man, and if two men ride of a horse, one must ride behind. Truthfully, he is as honest a soul as anyone who has ever eaten. But after all, God bless him, all men are not created equal, good neighbor!

Leonato Indeed, neighbor, he falls far short compared to you.

Dogberry These are gifts from God.

Leonato I have to leave you.

Dogberry   One word, sir. Our watch, sir, have indeed comprehended two aspicious persons, and we would have them this morning examin'd before your wor-
48   ship.

Leonato   Take their examination yourself, and bring it me. I am now in great haste, as it may appear
51   unto you.

Dogberry   It shall be suffigance.

Leonato   Drink some wine ere you go; fare you well.

[*Enter a* **Messenger**.]

Messenger   My lord, they stay for you to give your
55   daughter to her husband.

Leonato   I'll wait upon them, I am ready.

[*Exeunt Leonato and Messenger.*]

Dogberry   Go, good partner, go, get you to Francis Seacole, bid him bring his pen and inkhorn to the jail. We are now to examination these men.

60 **Verges**   And we must do it wisely.

Dogberry   We will spare for no wit, I warrant you. Here's that shall drive some of them to a non-come; only get the learned writer to set down our excommunication, and meet me at the jail.

[*Exeunt.*]

Dogberry   One more word, sir. Our watchmen sir, have indeed comprehended [*he means "apprehended"*] two aspicious [*he means "suspicious"*] persons, and we would like you to examine them this morning.

Leonato   Examine them yourself and bring the results to me. I am in a big hurry now, as it might appear obvious to you.

Dogberry   That will be suffigance [*he means "sufficient"*].

Leonato   Have some wine before you go, good-bye.

[*A **Messenger** enters.*]

Messenger   My lord, they are waiting for you to give your daughter to her husband.

Leonato   I'll be right there, I am ready.

[*Leonato and the messenger exit.*]

Dogberry   Go, good partner, go. Get Francis Seacoal and ask him to bring his pen and ink to the jail, where we will examination [*he means "examine"*] these men.

Verges   And we must do it wisely.

Dogberry   We will not spare any wisdom, I promise you. We will drive some of them to a noncome [*he means "to a state of perplexity"*], but get the learned writer to write down our excommunication [*he means "examination"*] and then meet me at the jail.

[*They exit.*]

Act four

Scene 1

Enter Prince [**Don Pedro**, **Don John** *the*] *Bastard,* **Leonato**, **Friar** [**Francis**], **Claudio**, **Benedick**, **Hero**, *and* **Beatrice** [*with* **Attendants**].

Leonato   Come, Friar Francis, be brief—only to the plain form of marriage, and you shall recount their particular duties afterwards.

Friar   You come hither, my lord, to marry this
5   lady.

Claudio   No.

Leonato   To be married to her. Friar, you come to marry her.

Friar   Lady, you come hither to be married to
10   this count.

Hero   I do.

Friar   If either of you know any inward impediment why you should not be conjoin'd, I charge you on your souls to utter it.

15 **Claudio**   Know you any, Hero?

Hero   None, my lord.

Friar   Know you any, Count?

Leonato   I dare make his answer, none.

Claudio   O, what men dare do! What men may do! What men daily do, not knowing what they do!

Act four

Scene 1

Enter **Don Pedro, Don John, Leonato, Friar Francis, Claudio, Benedick, Hero, Beatrice,** *and* **Attendants** *at a church.*

Leonato   All right, Friar Francis, be brief and keep the ceremony simple; you can explain their marriage duties later.

Friar Francis   [*to Claudio*] My lord, have you come here to marry this lady?

Claudio   No.

Leonato   He's to be married *to* her. Friar, you have come here to marry her.

Friar Francis   Lady, you come here to be married to this count.

Hero   I do.

Friar Francis   If either of you know any undisclosed reason why you should not be united, command your souls to announce it.

Claudio   Do you know of any, Hero?

Hero   None, my lord.

Friar Francis   Do you know of any, count?

Leonato   I can answer that for him, none.

Claudio   Oh, how dare you! What things that men are allowed to do, and what men do on a daily basis not knowing that they are doing it!

Benedick   How now! interjections? Why then, some
22   be of laughing, as, ah, ha, he!

Claudio   Stand thee by, friar. Father, by your leave,
Will you with free and unconstrained soul
25   Give me this maid, your daughter?

Leonato   As freely, son, as God did give her me.

Claudio   And what have I to give you back whose worth
May counterpoise this rich and precious gift?

Don Pedro   Nothing, unless you render her again.

30 **Claudio**   Sweet Prince, you learn me noble thankfulness.
There, Leonato, take her back again.
Give not this rotten orange to your friend,
She's but the sign and semblance of her honor.
Behold how like a maid she blushes here!
35   O, what authority and show of truth
Can cunning sin cover itself withal!
Comes not that blood as modest evidence
To witness simple virtue? Would you not swear,
All you that see her, that she were a maid,
40   By these exterior shows? But she is none:
She knows the heat of a luxurious bed;
Her blush is guiltiness, not modesty.

Leonato   What do you mean, my lord?

Claudio   Not to be married,
Not to knit my soul to an approved wanton.

Leonato   Dear my lord, if you, in your own proof,
46   Have vanquish'd the resistance of her youth,
And made defeat of her virginity—

Benedick   What's with the interjections? Why don't you add some of that demonstrative laughing as in "ah, ha, he!"?

Claudio   Step aside, Friar. Father, with your unrestrained permission will you give me this virgin, your daughter?

Leonato   Yes son, as freely as God gave her to me.

Claudio   And what can I give back to you that would equal this rich and precious gift?

Don Pedro   Nothing, except for grandchildren.

Claudio   Dear Prince, you have taught me to be gracious. There, Leonato, take her back. Don't give a rotting orange to a friend; she only appears to be honorable on the outside. Look how she is blushing! How daring and truthful does the devious sin disguise itself. Isn't blushing proof of a desirable quality? You would swear by looking at her that she was a virgin, but she isn't. She knows the passions of a lascivious bed. Her blush is from guilt, not from modesty.

Leonato   What do you mean, my lord?

Claudio   I will not be married nor unite my soul to a guilty and immoral woman.

Leonato   Please, my lord, if you have conquered her youthful resistance for your own proof and taken her virginity—

Claudio   I know what you would say. If I have known her,
You will say, she did embrace me as a husband,
50   And so extenuate the 'forehand sin.
No, Leonato,
I never tempted her with word too large,
But as a brother to his sister, show'd
Bashful sincerity and comely love.

55 **Hero**   And seem'd I ever otherwise to you?

Claudio   Out on thee seeming! I will write against it:
You seem to me as Dian in her orb,
As chaste as is the bud ere it be blown;
But you are more intemperate in your blood
60   Than Venus, or those pamp'red animals
That rage in savage sensuality.

Hero   Is my lord well, that he doth speak so wide?

Leonato   Sweet Prince, why speak not you?

Don Pedro   What should I speak?
I stand dishonor'd, that have gone about
65   To link my dear friend to a common stale.

Leonato   Are these things spoken, or do I but dream?

Don John   Sir, they are spoken, and these things are true.

Benedick   This looks not like a nuptial.

Hero   "True"! O God!

Claudio   Leonato, stand I here?
70   Is this the Prince? is this the Prince's brother?
Is this face Hero's? are our eyes our own?

Leonato   All this is so, but what of this, my lord?

Claudio   I knew you would say that if I had slept with her, that she embraced me as a husband and that excuses the premarital sin. No, Leonato, I never tempted her with improper words but treated her like a brother treats his sister, with shy sincerity and respectable love.

Hero   And did I ever seem otherwise to you?

Claudio   Curses on you! Seeming! To me you seemed like Diane [*Roman goddess of the hunt*] in her orbit and as innocent as a bud before it blossoms. But your sexual appetite is more excessive than Venus, or like a pampered animal that seethes in untamed sensuality.

Hero   Are you not feeling well, my lord? Is that causing you to speak so wildly?

Leonato   Dear Prince, why aren't you saying anything?

Don Pedro   What should I say? I have been dishonored to have united my dear friend to a common prostitute.

Leonato   Are these things real or am I dreaming?

Don John   Sir, they are real and true.

Benedick   This doesn't look like a wedding.

Hero   True? Oh God!

Claudio   Leonato, am I standing here? Is this the Prince? Is this the Prince's brother? Is this Hero's face? Are these our eyes?

Leonato   All this is true, but what is this all about, my lord?

Claudio   Let me but move one question to your daughter,
And by that fatherly and kindly power
75   That you have in her, bid her answer truly.

Leonato   I charge thee do so, as thou art my child.

Hero   O God defend me, how am I beset!
What kind of catechizing call you this?

Claudio   To make you answer truly to your name.

Hero   Is it not Hero? Who can blot that name
With any just reproach?

81 **Claudio**   Marry, that can Hero,
Hero itself can blot out Hero's virtue.
What man was he talk'd with you yesternight
Out at your window betwixt twelve and one?
85   Now, if you are a maid, answer to this.

Hero   I talk'd with no man at that hour, my lord.

Don Pedro   Why then are you no maiden. Leonato,
I am sorry you must hear. Upon mine honor,
Myself, my brother, and this grieved count
90   Did see her, hear her, at that hour last night
Talk with a ruffian at her chamber-window,
Who hath indeed, most like a liberal villain,
Confess'd the vile encounters they have had
A thousand times in secret.

95 **Don John**   Fie, fie, they are not to be named, my lord,
Not to be spoke of;
There is not chastity enough in language
Without offense to utter them. Thus, pretty lady,
I am sorry for thy much misgovernment.

Claudio   Let me ask only one question of your daughter, and with your kind and fatherly powers, ask her to answer it truthfully.

Leonato   My child, I order you to answer truthfully.

Hero   Oh God, please defend me! I am overwhelmed! What kind of interrogation is this?

Claudio   It is to force you to answer to your true name.

Hero   Isn't my name Hero? How can you tarnish that name with a mere accusation?

Claudio   By the Virgin Mary, Hero can. Hero can tarnish Hero's virtue herself. What man were you talking to last night at your bedroom window between twelve and one? If you are a virgin, answer this.

Hero   I didn't talk with any man at that hour, my lord.

Don Pedro   Well then, you are no virgin. Leonato, I am sorry that you have to hear this, but on my honor, we all heard her speaking with a ruffian last night at her bedroom window who confessed the thousands of secret encounters they have had.

Don John   No, no, do not speak of the offenses, there isn't any word inoffensive enough to describe them without offending everyone here. Pretty lady, I am ashamed of your indiscretions.

100 **Claudio**   O Hero! what a Hero hadst thou been,
　　　　If half thy outward graces had been placed
　　　　About thy thoughts and counsels of thy heart!
　　　　But fare thee well, most foul, most fair! Farewell,
　　　　Thou pure impiety and impious purity!
105　　For thee I'll lock up all the gates of love,
　　　　And on my eyelids shall conjecture hang,
　　　　To turn all beauty into thoughts of harm,
　　　　And never shall it more be gracious.

　　Leonato   Hath no man's dagger here a point for me?

　　　　　　　　　　　　　　　　　　　　[*Hero swoons.*]

110 **Beatrice**   Why, how now, cousin, wherefore sink you down?

　　Don John   Come, let us go. These things, come thus to light,
　　Smother her spirits up.

　　　　　　　　[*Exeunt Don Pedro, Don John, and Claudio.*]

　　Benedick   How doth the lady?

　　Beatrice   Dead, I think. Help, uncle!
　　Hero, why, Hero! Uncle! Signior Benedick! Friar!

115 **Leonato**   O Fate! take not away thy heavy hand.
　　　　Death is the fairest cover for her shame
　　　　That may be wish'd for.

　　Beatrice　　　　　　　　How now, cousin Hero!

　　Friar   Have comfort, lady.

　　Leonato   Dost thou look up?

　　Friar　　　　　　　　Yea, wherefore should she not?

Claudio   Oh Hero, what a Hero you might have been, if only outward beauty matched the thoughts and desires of your heart! Good-bye, most wicked and most beautiful. Good-bye to your pure sinfulness and immoral purity! Because of you I will keep myself from love and will be suspicious of all beauty that I see, turning those visions into harmful thoughts, and always be grateful for that.

Leonato   Isn't there anyone with a dagger for me?

[*Hero collapses.*]

Beatrice   What's wrong, cousin, why have you fallen?

Don John   Come on, let's go. These disclosures have over-whelmed her spirit.

[*Don Pedro, Don John, and Claudio exit.*]

Benedick   How is she?

Beatrice   Dead, I think. Uncle, help! Hero! Why Hero? Uncle! Signior Benedick! Friar!

Leonato   Oh Fate! Do not spare her from this punishment. Death would be the kindest way to cover her shame that could ever happen.

Beatrice   How are you now, Hero?

Friar Francis   Take comfort, lady.

Leonato   Are you looking up?

Friar Francis   Yes, why shouldn't she?

120 **Leonato**   Wherefore? why, doth not every earthly thing
Cry shame upon her? could she here deny
The story that is printed in her blood?
Do not live, Hero, do not ope thine eyes;
124 For did I think thou wouldst not quickly die,
Thought I thy spirits were stronger than thy shames,
Myself would, on the rearward of reproaches,
Strike at thy life. Griev'd I, I had but one?
Chid I for that at frugal nature's frame?
O, one too much by thee! Why had I one?
130 Why ever wast thou lovely in my eyes?
Why had I not with charitable hand
Took up a beggar's issue at my gates,
Who smirched thus and mir'd with infamy,
I might have said, "No part of it is mine;
135 This shame derives itself from unknown loins"?
But mine, and mine I lov'd and mine I prais'd,
And mine that I was proud on, mine so much
That I myself was to myself not mine,
Valuing of her—why, she, O, she is fall'n
140 Into a pit of ink, that the wide sea
Hath drops too few to wash her clean again,
And salt too little which may season give
To her foul tainted flesh!

Benedick   Sir, sir, be patient.
For my part I am so attir'd in wonder,
145 I know not what to say.

Beatrice   O, on my soul, my cousin is belied!

Benedick   Lady, were you her bedfellow last night?

Beatrice   No, truly, not, although until last night,
I have this twelvemonth been her bedfellow.

Leonato   Why! Why, isn't everything on earth shaming her?
Can she deny the accusations that are proven so obvious
with her blushing? Don't live, Hero. Don't open your eyes.
If I didn't think that you would die quickly and believed that
your spirits were strong enough to withstand your shame
after this public scandal, I would kill you myself. I am sorry
that I had only one child, and I blame nature for being so
thrifty. Oh, but with you, one is too much. Why did I have
only one child? What did I ever see that was so lovely about
you? I should have been more charitable and adopted a
beggar's child that was left at my doorstep. I could have
denied that it was my child if it had shamed me like this.
But you were mine, and I loved you because you were
mine, and I praised you and was proud that you were mine
so much so that I hardly took time for myself because I
loved you so much. Now she has fallen into a pit of ink that
even the wide sea doesn't have enough water to wash her
clean with and too little salt to season her impure flesh!

Benedick   Sir, sir, be patient. As for me, I am so bewildered
by it all that I don't know what to say.

Beatrice   Oh, on my soul, my cousin has been slandered!

Benedick   Lady, did you sleep in her room last night?

Beatrice   No, I didn't, but honestly up until last night, I've
stayed in her room for the past twelve months.

150 **Leonato** Confirm'd, confirm'd! O, that is stronger made
  Which was before barr'd up with ribs of iron!
  Would the two princes lie, and Claudio lie,
  Who lov'd her so, that speaking of her foulness,
  Wash'd it with tears? Hence from her, let her die.

155 **Friar** Hear me a little,
  For I have only been silent so long,
  And given way unto this course of fortune,
  By noting of the lady. I have mark'd
159 A thousand blushing apparitions
  To start into her face, a thousand innocent shames
  In angel whiteness beat away those blushes,
  And in her eye there hath appear'd a fire
  To burn the errors that these princes hold
  Against her maiden truth. Call me a fool,
165 Trust not my reading, nor my observations,
  Which with experimental seal doth warrant
  The tenure of my book; trust not my age,
  My reverence, calling, nor divinity,
  If this sweet lady lie not guiltless here
  Under some biting error.

170 **Leonato**   Friar, it cannot be.
  Thou seest that all the grace that she hath left
  Is that she will not add to her damnation
  A sin of perjury; she not denies it.
  Why seek'st thou then to cover with excuse
175 That which appears in proper nakedness?

  Friar Lady, what man is he you are accus'd of?

Leonato   Proof? That's proof? Oh, that proves their accusations, which were strong in the beginning, are now indisputable. Would either of the two princes lie? Would Claudio lie—the one who loved her so much that speaking of her uncleanness caused him to cry? Get away from her! Let her die.

Friar Francis   Listen to me awhile; I have been quiet and have accepted these events for too long. Because I have been watching the lady's reaction, I've noticed her begin to blush a thousand times, but an angelic paleness overwhelmed those blushes. In her eyes, there is a fire intent on burning away the lies that the princes have told about her chastity. You can call me a fool if I am wrong, and you don't have to trust my observations, which are underscored by my experience as a friar. You don't have to trust my age, my reverence, vocation, or spirituality. But this sweet lady is not guilty.

Leonato   Friar, this cannot be. Can't you see that the only dignity she has left is to not add lying to her list of sins for damnation? She doesn't deny the accusations. Why would you try to excuse her from something that appears so obvious?

Friar Francis   Lady, who is the man that you are accused of being with?

Hero They know that do accuse me, I know none.
If I know more of any man alive
Than that which maiden modesty doth warrant,
180 Let all my sins lack mercy! O my father,
Prove you that any man with me convers'd
At hours unmeet, or that I yesternight
Maintain'd the change of words with any creature,
Refuse me, hate me, torture me to death!

185 **Friar** There is some strange misprision in the princes.

Benedick Two of them have the very bent of honor,
And if their wisdoms be misled in this,
The practice of it lives in John the Bastard,
189 Whose spirits toil in frame of villainies.

Leonato I know not. If they speak but truth of her,
These hands shall tear her; if they wrong her honor,
The proudest of them shall well hear of it.
Time hath not yet so dried this blood of mine,
Nor age so eat up my invention,
195 Nor fortune made such havoc of my means,
Nor my bad life reft me so much of friends,
But they shall find, awak'd in such a kind,
Both strength of limb and policy of mind,
Ability in means and choice of friends,
To quit me of them throughly.

200 **Friar**   Pause awhile,
And let my counsel sway you in this case.
Your daughter here the [princes] left for dead,
Let her awhile be secretly kept in,
And publish it that she is dead indeed.
205 Maintain a mourning ostentation,
And on your family's old monument
Hang mournful epitaphs, and do all rites
That appertain unto a burial.

Hero   Only they know that answer, I don't know what they are talking about. If there is any man alive that I have behaved improperly with, then let all of my sins be punished to the fullest. Father, if you can prove that any man met with me last night and that I exchanged words with anyone, disown me, hate me, and torture me to death!

Friar Francis   There has to be some strange misunderstanding with the princes.

Benedick   Two of them are completely honorable, and if their good judgments are deceived, then it has to be blamed on John the bastard, whose strength lies in plotting wrongdoings.

Leonato   I don't know. If they are telling the truth about her, I will tear her apart with my bare hands, but if they have erroneously dishonored her, the haughtier of the two will have to deal with me. Age hasn't deteriorated my body nor has it destroyed my wisdom. Fortune has not been my enemy nor has a bad life limited my friendships. The princes will find a man who is strong in both mind and body, and with the ability in both wealth and choice of friends to help me pay them back completely.

Friar Francis   Let's wait awhile, and let my suggestion change your mind in this. When the princes left, they thought your daughter was as good as dead. Secretly keep her hidden inside and make it known that she is dead. Pretend to be in mourning and hang mournful epitaphs on your family's monument and do everything in keeping with a real burial.

Leonato   What shall become of this? what will this do?

Friar   Marry, this well carried shall on her behalf
211   Change slander to remorse; that is some good.
But not for that dream I on this strange course,
But on this travail look for greater birth:
She dying, as it must so be maintain'd,
215   Upon the instant that she was accus'd,
Shall be lamented, pitied and excus'd
Of every hearer; for it so falls out
That what we have we prize not to the worth
Whiles we enjoy it, but being lack'd and lost,
220   Why then we rack the value; then we find
The virtue that possession would not show us
Whiles it was ours. So will it fare with Claudio:
When he shall hear she died upon his words,
Th' idea of her life shall sweetly creep
225   Into his study of imagination,
And every lovely organ of her life
Shall come apparell'd in more precious habit,
More moving, delicate, and full of life,
229   Into the eye and prospect of his soul,
Than when she liv'd indeed. Then shall he mourn,
If ever love had interest in his liver,
And wish he had not so accused her;
No, though he thought his accusation true.
Let this be so, and doubt not but success
235   Will fashion the event in better shape
Than I can lay it down in likelihood.
But if all aim but this be levell'd false,
The supposition of the lady's death
Will quench the wonder of her infamy.
240   And if it sort not well, you may conceal her,
As best befits her wounded reputation,
In some reclusive and religious life,
Out of all eyes, tongues, minds, and injuries.

Leonato   What is going to be the result of all of this? How is this going to help?

Friar Francis   I promise, if this is carried out well, it will change slander to remorse on her behalf, and that is good. But there is a more important goal for this unusual course of action. We will say that she died the minute she was accused, and everyone will grieve over her, pity her, and excuse her alleged actions. Everyone will realize that we take things we love for granted, but once they are lost we understand their value to us. This is how it will be with Claudio. When he hears that she died because of his words, the memories of her life will creep into his conscience. And everything beautiful about her will become more apparent and more dear, more delicate and full of life in his mind, even more so than when she was alive. He will mourn and regret that he accused her, even though he believed his accusations to be true. Give it a try, I know it will work. The playing out of the events will no doubt end far better than I've described. Hero's alleged death will end the extensive damage to her reputation. And, if it doesn't end well, then you can keep her hidden and pledge her to life in a nunnery, which will keep her away from all eyes, gossip, thoughts, and insults.

Benedick   Signior Leonato, let the friar advise you,
245   And though you know my inwardness and love
Is very much unto the Prince and Claudio,
Yet, by mine honor, I will deal in this
As secretly and justly as your soul
Should with your body.

Leonato   Being that I flow in grief,
250   The smallest twine may lead me.

Friar   'Tis well consented; presently away,
For to strange sores strangely they strain the cure.
Come, lady, die to live; this wedding-day
Perhaps is but prolong'd, have patience and endure.

Exit [with all but Benedick and Beatrice].

Benedick   Lady Beatrice, have you wept all this while?

256 **Beatrice**   Yea, and I will weep a while longer.

Benedick   I will not desire that.

Beatrice   You have no reason, I do it freely.

Benedick   Surely I do believe your fair cousin is
260   wrong'd.

Beatrice   Ah, how much might the man deserve of me
that would right her!

Benedick   Is there any way to show such friendship?

Beatrice   A very even way, but no such friend.

265 **Benedick**   May a man do it?

Beatrice   It is a man's office, but not yours.

Benedick   I do love nothing in the world so well as
268   you—is not that strange?

Benedick Signior Leonato, take the friar's advice. And even though you know that I have a close friendship and love with the Prince and Claudio, I promise that I will keep this just as secretly and as justly as you should.

Leonato Because I am so immersed in grief, the smallest thread of hope will guide me right now.

Friar Francis You are doing the right thing, now go away immediately. We have to heal unusual wounds in unusual ways. Go lady, you have to die to live. The wedding day is perhaps only postponed—you need to have patience and endurance.

[*Everyone exits except Benedick and Beatrice.*]

Benedick Lady Beatrice, have you been crying the entire time?

Beatrice Yes, and I will continue to cry.

Benedick I don't want you to.

Beatrice You don't have to, I cry at my own free will.

Benedick Honestly, I believe your cousin is being victimized.

Beatrice Ah, I will owe the man who avenges her more than I can say.

Benedick Is there any way that I can show such friendship?

Beatrice There is a very straightforward way, but it is not for a friend.

Benedick Would a man be able to do it?

Beatrice It is a man's job, but not yours.

Benedick I love nothing in the world as much as I love you, isn't that strange?

Beatrice   As strange as the thing I know not. It were as possible for me to say I lov'd nothing so well as you, but believe me not; and yet I lie not: I confess nothing, nor I deny nothing. I am sorry for my cousin.

Benedick   By my sword, Beatrice, thou lovest me.

275 **Beatrice**   Do not swear and eat it.

Benedick   I will swear by it that you love me, and I will make him eat it that says I love not you.

Beatrice   Will you not eat your word?

Benedick   With no sauce that can be devis'd to it. I
280   protest I love thee.

Beatrice   Why then God forgive me!

Benedick   What offense, sweet Beatrice?

Beatrice   You have stay'd me in a happy hour, I was about to protest I lov'd you.

285 **Benedick**   And do it with all thy heart.

Beatrice   I love you with so much of my heart that none is left to protest.

Benedick   Come, bid me do any thing for thee.

Beatrice   Kill Claudio.

290 **Benedick**   Ha, not for the wide world.

Beatrice   You kill me to deny it. Farewell.

Benedick   Tarry, sweet Beatrice.

Beatrice   I am gone, though I am here; there is no love in you. Nay, I pray you let me go.

Beatrice   It is as strange as this event that I don't under-stand. It is certainly possible for me to say that I love nothing as much as you, but don't believe me, even though I am not lying. I won't confess anything, nor do I deny any-thing. I feel so sorry for my cousin.

Benedick   By my sword, Beatrice, you love me.

Beatrice   Do not swear by it and then have to go back and eat your words.

Benedick   I will swear that you love me, and I will make anyone eat it that says I don't love you.

Beatrice   Then you won't eat your words?

Benedick   Not with any sauce that they could add to make them tastier. I swear I love you.

Beatrice   Why, then, God forgive me!

Benedick   For what, sweet Beatrice?

Beatrice   You managed to stop me at a fortunate time, because I was about to swear that I loved you.

Benedick   Then do it with all your heart.

Beatrice   I love you with so much of my heart that there is nothing left to swear with.

Benedick   Please, ask me to do anything for you.

Beatrice   Kill Claudio.

Benedick   Ha! I wouldn't do that for the entire world.

Beatrice   Then you kill me to refuse. Good-bye.

Benedick   Stay, sweet Beatrice.

Beatrice   I am gone even though you are making me stay. You don't love me, no, please let me go.

295 **Benedick**   Beatrice—

Beatrice   In faith, I will go.

Benedick   We'll be friends first.

Beatrice   You dare easier be friends with me than fight with mine enemy.

300 **Benedick**   Is Claudio thine enemy?

Beatrice   Is 'a not approv'd in the height a villain, that hath slander'd, scorn'd, dishonor'd my kins-woman? O that I were a man! What, bear her in

304 hand until they come to take hands, and then with public accusation, uncover'd slander, unmitigated rancor—O God, that I were a man! I would eat his heart in the market-place.

Benedick   Hear me, Beatrice—

Beatrice   Talk with a man out at a window! a proper

310 saying!

Benedick   Nay, but, Beatrice—

Beatrice   Sweet Hero, she is wrong'd, she is sland'red, she is undone.

Benedick   Beat—

Beatrice   Princes and counties! Surely a princely

316 testimony, a goodly count, Count Comfect, a sweet gallant surely! O that I were a man for his sake! or that I had any friend would be a man for my sake! But manhood is melted into cur'sies, valor into compli-

320 ment, and men are only turn'd into tongue, and trim ones too. He is now as valiant as Hercules that only tells a lie, and swears it. I cannot be a man with wishing, therefore I will die a woman with grieving.

Benedick Beatrice—

Beatrice Honestly, I want to go.

Benedick Not until we are friends again.

Beatrice Do you think it is easier to be friends with me than fight with my enemy?

Benedick Is Claudio your enemy?

Beatrice Hasn't he proved that he is the epitome of an enemy after he slandered, scorned, and dishonored my cousin? Oh, if only I were a man! How could he pretend everything was fine until they were to exchange vows, and then publicly accuse her, reveal slander, absolute malice— oh God, if only I were a man! I would eat his heart in the marketplace.

Benedick Listen to me Beatrice—

Beatrice She was talking with a man at her window! That's a likely story!

Benedick No, but, Beatrice—

Beatrice Sweet Hero! She is victimized, she is slandered, and she is ruined.

Benedick Beat—

Beatrice Princes and counts! That was sure a princely testimony. Oh, the honest count, Count Candy, such a sweet gentleman, indeed! Oh, if only I were a man because of him, or if only I had a friend that would be a man for my sake! But manhood has been melted into politeness, bravery into compliments—and men have become fine, elegant talkers who are as brave as Hercules who tells lies and swears by it. I cannot become a man through wishing; therefore, I'll have to die a grieving woman.

181

Benedick   Tarry, good Beatrice. By this hand, I love
325   thee.

Beatrice   Use it for my love some other way than
swearing by it.

Benedick   Think you in your soul the Count Claudio
hath wrong'd Hero?

330 **Beatrice**   Yea, as sure as I have a thought or a soul.

Benedick   Enough, I am engag'd, I will challenge
him. I will kiss your hand, and so I leave you. By
this hand, Claudio shall render me a dear account.
As you hear of me, so think of me. Go comfort
your cousin. I must say she is dead; and so, fare-
336   well.

[Exeunt.]

Scene 2

*Enter the Constables [**Dogberry** and **Verges**] and the Town
Clerk [or **Sexton**] in gowns, [and the **Watch** with **Conrade**
and] **Borachio**.*

Dogberry   Is our whole dissembly appear'd?

Verges   O, a stool and a cushion for the sexton.

Sexton   Which be the malefactors?

Dogberry   Marry, that am I and my partner.

Verges   Nay, that's certain, we have the exhibition
6   to examine.

Benedick Stay, good Beatrice. I swear with this hand that I love you.

Beatrice Then use your hand for my love in some other way than swearing by it.

Benedick Do you really think in your soul that Count Claudio has wronged Hero?

Beatrice Yes, as sure as I have a thought or a soul.

Benedick That's enough for me; I am committed and will challenge him. I will kiss your hand and leave you. Claudio will pay dearly because of this hand. As you hear me now, keep me in your thoughts. Go take care of your cousin; I must tell them that she is dead. Good-bye.

[*They exit.*]

Scene 2

Enter **Dogberry**, **Verges**, *and* **Sexton**, *in official black gowns, and the* **Watch**, *with* **Conrade** *and* **Borachio**, *in a prison.*

Dogberry Is our whole dissembly [*he means "assembly"*] here?

Verges Oh, we need a stool and cushion for the sexton.

Sexton Which of these are the criminals?

Dogberry Sir, that would be me and my partner.

Verges Yes, that's certain; we have been exhibitioned [*he means "commissioned"*] to examine this case.

Sexton   But which are the offenders that are to be
examin'd? Let them come before Master Constable.

Dogberry   Yea, marry, let them come before me.
10   What is your name, friend?

Borachio   Borachio.

Dogberry   Pray write down Borachio. Yours, sirrah?

Conrade   I am a gentleman, sir, and my name is
Conrade.

Dogberry   Write down Master Gentleman Conrade.
16   Masters, do you serve God?

Both [Conrade, Borachio]   Yea, sir, we hope.

Dogberry   Write down, that they hope they serve God;
and write God first, for God defend but God should
20   go before such villains! Masters, it is prov'd
already that you are little better than false knaves,
and it will go near to be thought so shortly. How
answer you for yourselves?

24 **Conrade**   Marry, sir, we say we are none.

Dogberry   A marvellous witty fellow, I assure you,
but I will go about with him. Come you hither,
sirrah; a word in your ear, sir. I say to you, it is
thought you are false knaves.

29 **Borachio**   Sir, I say to you, we are none.

Dogberry   Well, stand aside. 'Fore God, they are
both in a tale. Have you writ down, that they are
none?

Sexton   Master Constable, you go not the way to
examine; you must call forth the watch that are
35   their accusers.

Sexton   But which of these are the offenders that I need to examine? Bring them before the master constable.

Dogberry   Yes, of course, sir, bring them before me. What is your name, friend?

Borachio   Borachio.

Dogberry   Please, write down, Borachio. And your name sir?

Conrade   I am a gentleman, sir, and my name is Conrade.

Dogberry   Write down, master gentleman Conrade. Masters, do you serve God?

Conrade and Borachio   Yes, sir, we hope.

Dogberry   Write down, that they hope they serve God, and make sure you write God first, God help us if we put criminals ahead of God. Masters, it is already known that you are nothing more than liars, and that will be proven shortly. How do you both plead?

Conrade   Truly, sir, we are not criminals.

Dogberry   What a clever man, that's for certain, but I will set to work on him. Come here, sir, let me whisper in your ear: Sir, I am telling you that we think you are liars.

Borachio   Sir, and I am telling you that we are not.

Dogberry   Well, stand aside. Before God, they are both telling the same story. Have you written it down that they are not liars?

Sexton   Master constable, that is not the way to examine the criminals; you must call the watchmen forward, the men who accuse them.

Dogberry   Yea, marry, that's the eftest way; let the
watch come forth. Masters, I charge you in the
Prince's name accuse these men.

1st Watchman   This man said, sir, that Don John,
40   the Prince's brother, was a villain.

Dogberry   Write down Prince John a villain. Why,
this is flat perjury, to call a prince's brother villain.

Borachio   Master Constable—

Dogberry   Pray thee, fellow, peace. I do not like thy
45   look, I promise thee.

Sexton   What heard you him say else?

2nd Watchman   Marry, that he had receiv'd a thousand ducats of Don John for accusing the Lady Hero
wrongfully.

50 **Dogberry**   Flat burglary as ever was committed.

Verges   Yea, by mass, that it is.

Sexton   What else, fellow?

1st Watchman   And that Count Claudio did mean,
upon his words, to disgrace Hero before the whole
55   assembly, and not marry her.

Dogberry   O villain! thou wilt be condemn'd into ever-
lasting redemption for this.

Sexton   What else?

59 **1st and 2nd Watchmen**   This is all.

Dogberry   Yes, of course, that's the eftest [*he means "deftest" or "fastest"*] way. Bring the watchmen forward. Masters, I charge you in the name of the Prince, accuse these men.

First Watchman   Sir, this man said that Don John, the Prince's brother, is a villain.

Dogberry   Write down, that Prince John is a villain. Why, this is out and out perjury [*he means "treachery"*] to call a prince's brother a villain.

Borachio   Master constable,—

Dogberry   Please, be quiet. I do not like the look of you, I promise you.

Sexton   What else did you hear him say?

Second Watchman   Yes, that he had received a thousand pieces of gold from Don John for wrongfully accusing Lady Hero.

Dogberry   That's the worst robbery that has ever been committed.

Verges   Yes, by God, it really is.

Sexton   What else, fellow?

First Watchman   And that Count Claudio intended to disgrace Hero in front of the entire congregation and not marry her.

Dogberry   What a villain! You will be condemned to eternal redemption [*he means "damnation"*] for this.

Sexton   What else?

Watchmen   That is all.

Sexton   And this is more, masters, than you can deny.
Prince John is this morning secretly stol'n away. Hero
was in this manner accus'd, in this very manner
refus'd, and upon the grief of this suddenly died.
Master Constable, let these men be bound, and brought
to Leonato's. I will go before and show him their
66   examination.

                                                    [*Exit.*]

Dogberry   Come let them be opinion'd.

Verges   Let them be in the hands—

Conrade   [Off,] coxcomb!

70 **Dogberry**   God's my life, where's the sexton? Let
him write down the Prince's officer coxcomb. Come,
bind them. Thou naughty varlet!

Conrade   Away, you are an ass, you are an ass.

Dogberry   Dost thou not suspect my place? Dost thou
75   not suspect my years? O that he were here to
write me down an ass! But, masters, remember that
I am an ass; though it be not written down, yet forget
not that I am an ass. No, thou villain, thou art full of
piety, as shall be prov'd upon thee by good witness.
80   I am a wise fellow, and which is more, an officer,
and which is more, a householder, and which is more,
as pretty a piece of flesh as any is in Messina, and
one that knows the law, go to, and a rich fellow
enough, go to, and a fellow that hath had losses, and
85   one that hath two gowns, and every thing handsome about him. Bring him away. O that I had been
writ down an ass!

                                                    Exeunt.

Sexton   Master, this is more than you can deny. This morning, Prince John secretly left the area. Hero was accused exactly as it is described here and, being refused in marriage, suddenly died. Master constable, tie these men up and bring them to Leonato's. I will go ahead of you and show him their examination.

[*He exits.*]

Dogberry   Come, let them be opinioned [*he means "pinioned" — to be bound*].

Verges   Tie them at their hands—

Conrade   Get off, you fool!

Dogberry   With God as my witness, where's the sexton? He should write down that the Prince's officer is a fool. Come on, tie them up. You are a wicked rascal!

Conrade   Get away! You are an ass, you are an ass!

Dogberry   Do you not suspect [*he means "respect"*] my position? Do you not suspect [*he means "respect"*] my age? Oh, if only the sexton were here to write down that I am an ass! But, masters, remember that I am an ass even though it is not written down. No, you villain, you are full of piety [*he means "impiety"*], as will be proven about you with honest witnesses. I am wise, and more importantly, an officer, and even more importantly, I am a householder, but even more importantly than that, I am as handsome as any piece of flesh in Messina and someone who knows the law, get going; and I'm rich enough, get going; I used to have more, but I have two sets of clothes and lovely things around me. Take him away. Oh, if only I had been written down as an ass!

[*They all exit.*]

Act five

Scene 1

Enter **Leonato** *and his brother* [**Antonio**].

Antonio   If you go on thus, you will kill yourself,
And 'tis not wisdom thus to second grief
Against yourself.

Leonato   I pray thee cease thy counsel,
Which falls into mine ears as profitless
5   As water in a sieve. Give not me counsel,
Nor let no comforter delight mine ear
But such a one whose wrongs do suit with mine.
Bring me a father that so lov'd his child,
Whose joy of her is overwhelm'd like mine,
10   And bid him speak of patience;
Measure his woe the length and breadth of mine,
And let it answer every strain for strain,
As thus for thus, and such a grief for such,
In every lineament, branch, shape, and form;
15   If such a one will smile and stroke his beard,
And, sorrow wag, cry "hem!" when he should groan,
Patch grief with proverbs, make misfortune drunk
With candle-wasters, bring him yet to me,
And I of him will gather patience.
20   But there is no such man, for, brother, men
Can counsel and speak comfort to that grief
Which they themselves not feel, but tasting it,
Their counsel turns to passion, which before
Would give preceptial med'cine to rage,
25   Fetter strong madness in a silken thread,
Charm ache with air, and agony with words.
No, no, 'tis all men's office to speak patience

Act five

Scene 1

Leonato *and* **Antonio** *enter in front of Leonato's house.*

Antonio   If you go on like this, you're going to kill yourself. Adding to your grief is not wise.

Leonato   Please, stop advising me, which means as much to me as water in a sieve. Don't advise me or try to comfort me. The only person who can comfort me is someone who has been wronged like I have. Bring me a father who loved his child so much and whose joy of her overwhelmed him like mine and ask him to be patient. Compare his grief with the length and breadth of mine. Compare his sadness, his complaints, and the intense emotions running through our bodies. If this man smiles, strokes his beard the way that you do, and says "ahem" when he should be groaning or tries to mend sorrow with proverbs, and bewilders misfortune with candle-wasters, then bring him to me and I will gather patience from him. But there is no such man. Brother, men can address grief and try to comfort, but those who have not experienced this pain cannot feel the depth of its passion. You cannot confine insanity with silken threads or charm an ache with hot air and agony with words. No, it is every man's obligation to speak of patience

To those that wring under the load of sorrow,
But no man's virtue nor sufficiency
30   To be so moral when he shall endure
The like himself. Therefore give me no counsel,
My griefs cry louder than advertisement.

Antonio   Therein do men from children nothing differ.

Leonato   I pray thee, peace. I will be flesh and blood,
35   For there was never yet philosopher
That could endure the toothache patiently,
However they have writ the style of gods,
And made a push at chance and sufferance.

Antonio   Yet bend not all the harm upon yourself;
40   Make those that do offend you suffer too.

Leonato   There thou speak'st reason; nay, I will do so.
My soul doth tell me Hero is belied,
And that shall Claudio know; so shall the Prince,
44   And all of them that thus dishonor her.

Enter Prince [**Don Pedro**] *and* **Claudio**.

Antonio   Here comes the Prince and Claudio hastily.

Don Pedro   Good den, good den.

Claudio   Good day to both of you.

Leonato   Hear you, my lords—

Don Pedro   We have some haste, Leonato.

Leonato   Some haste, my lord! Well, fare you well, my lord.
Are you so hasty now? well, all is one.

50 **Don Pedro**   Nay, do not quarrel with us, good old man.

Antonio   If he could right himself with quarrelling,
Some of us would lie low.

to those that are writhing under the burden of sorrow, but no one has the strength or the ability to moralize in that manner unless he has endured the same thing. Do not give me advice. My sorrows are more painful than what can be soothed with instructions.

Antonio   Then it seems that men are not at all different than children.

Leonato   Please, leave me be. I intend to be human. There has never been a philosopher that could tolerate a toothache patiently, although they write in a style worthy of gods and make an attack on chance and suffering.

Antonio   Don't endure all of the pain by yourself; make those that have wronged you suffer as well.

Leonato   There, now you are making sense; of course I will do that. My soul tells me that Hero has been lied about. Claudio will hear about it and the Prince and anyone else that disgraces her.

Antonio   Here come the Prince and Claudio in a hurry.

[**Don Pedro** and **Claudio** enter.]

Don Pedro   Good day, good day.

Claudio   Good day to both of you.

Leonato   Have you heard, my lords—

Don Pedro   We are in a hurry, Leonato.

Leonato   In a hurry, my lord! Well, good-bye my lord. Are you in such a hurry because it does not matter?

Don Pedro   Not at all, but do not argue with us, good old man.

Antonio   If he could avenge himself with arguing, there are a few of us who would die.

Claudio   Who wrongs him?

Leonato   Marry, thou dost wrong me, thou dissembler, thou—
Nay, never lay thy hand upon thy sword,
I fear thee not.

55 **Claudio**   Marry, beshrew my hand,
If it should give your age such cause of fear.
In faith, my hand meant nothing to my sword.

Leonato   Tush, tush, man, never fleer and jest at me;
I speak not like a dotard nor a fool,
60   As under privilege of age to brag
What I have done being young, or what would do
Were I not old. Know, Claudio, to thy head,
Thou hast so wrong'd mine innocent child and me
That I am forc'd to lay my reverence by,
65   And with grey hairs and bruise of many days,
Do challenge thee to trial of a man.
I say thou hast belied mine innocent child!
Thy slander hath gone through and through her heart,
And she lies buried with her ancestors—
70   O, in a tomb where never scandal slept,
Save this of hers, fram'd by thy villainy!

Claudio   My villainy?

Leonato   Thine, Claudio, thine, I say.

Don Pedro   You say not right, old man.

Leonato   My lord, my lord,
I'll prove it on his body, if he dare,
75   Despite his nice fence and his active practice,
His May of youth and bloom of lustihood.

Claudio   Away, I will not have to do with you.

Claudio   Who wrongs him?

Leonato   Indeed, you wrong me, you fake—you. Go ahead and try to frighten me by placing your hand on your sword; I'm not afraid of you.

Claudio   Excuse me, curse my hand if it would ever cause such fear in someone your age. Truthfully, I wasn't going to use my sword.

Leonato   Hush up, man—don't ever jeer or mock me. I'm not a weak-minded or foolish old man who has the privilege to brag about what I did when I was young or what I would do if I weren't so old. But I am telling you to your face, Claudio, you have so wronged my innocent child and me that I am forced to set aside my old man's respectability, with all of my grey hairs and aches of old age, and challenge you to a duel. I tell you that you have lied about my innocent child, and your insults have broken her heart. Now she is buried with her ancestors in a tomb where there has never been a scandal besides hers, all because of your vicious actions!

Claudio   My vicious actions?

Leonato   Yours, Claudio; yours, I say.

Don Pedro   You are wrong, old man.

Leonato   My lord, my lord, I'll prove his guilt on his body if he dares to accept my challenge, despite his elegant fencing skills and swordplay, his youth and air of manliness.

Claudio   Go away! I will have nothing to do with you.

Leonato Canst thou so daff me? Thou hast kill'd my child.
If thou kill'st me, boy, thou shalt kill a man.

80 **Antonio** He shall kill two of us, and men indeed;
But that's no matter, let him kill one first.
Win me and wear me, let him answer me.
Come, follow me, boy; come, sir boy, come follow me.
Sir boy, I'll whip you from your foining fence,
85 Nay, as I am a gentleman, I will.

Leonato Brother—

Antonio Content yourself. God knows I lov'd my niece,
And she is dead, slander'd to death by villains,
That dare as well answer a man indeed
90 As I dare take a serpent by the tongue.
Boys, apes, braggarts, Jacks, milksops!

Leonato   Brother Anthony—

Antonio Hold you content. What, man! I know them, yea,
And what they weigh, even to the utmost scruple—
Scrambling, outfacing, fashion-monging boys,
95 That lie and cog and flout, deprave and slander,
Go anticly, and show outward hideousness,
And speak [off] half a dozen dang'rous words,
How they might hurt their enemies—if they durst—
And this is all.

Leonato But, brother Anthony—

Antonio   Come, 'tis no matter;
101 Do not you meddle, let me deal in this.

Don Pedro Gentlemen both, we will not wake your patience.
My heart is sorry for your daughter's death;
But on my honor she was charg'd with nothing
105 But what was true, and very full of proof.

Leonato   Do you think you can be rid of me that easily? You have killed my child. If you kill me, boy, then you will have killed a man.

Antonio   He'll have to kill both of us, both men indeed. But that doesn't matter, let him kill one first, defeat one and then boast about it, and then let him fight with me. Come on boy, follow me—come, sir boy, come follow me. Sir boy, I'll whip you from your sword's thrust, indeed, as I am a gentleman, I will.

Leonato   Brother—

Antonio   Quiet. God knows I loved my niece and now she is dead, slandered to death by villains that would be just as likely to fight a real man as I would grab a poisonous snake by the tongue—boys, liars, braggarts, scoundrels, and wimps.

Leonato   Brother Anthony—

Antonio   Hold your comments. What kind of men are these? I know exactly who they are, and what they are made of down to the last ounce. They are contentious, brazen, fashion-following boys that lie, cheat, flout, vilify, and slander. They are dressed grotesquely, look terrifying, and talk only of how they might hurt their enemies if they dare to, and this is all.

Leonato   But, brother Anthony—

Antonio   Come on, it's not a big deal. Don't interfere, let me deal with this.

Don Pedro   Both of you gentlemen, we will not add to your troubles any longer. I am very sorry for your daughter's death, but on my honor, she was accused of nothing that was untrue or unproven.

Leonato   My lord, my lord—

Don Pedro   I will not hear you.

Leonato   No? Come, brother, away! I will be heard.

Antonio   And shall, or some of us will smart for it.

Exeunt ambo [*Leonato and Antonio*].

Enter **Benedick**.

110 **Don Pedro**   See, see, here comes the man we went to seek.

Claudio   Now, signior, what news?

Benedick   Good day, my lord.

Don Pedro   Welcome, signior, you are almost come
114   to part almost a fray.

Claudio   We had lik'd to have had our two noses
snapp'd off with two old men without teeth.

Don Pedro   Leonato and his brother. What think'st
thou? Had we fought, I doubt we should have been
too young for them.

Benedick   In a false quarrel there is no true valor.
121   I came to seek you both.

Claudio   We have been up and down to seek thee,
for we are high-proof melancholy, and would fain
have it beaten away. Wilt thou use thy wit?

125 **Benedick**   It is in my scabbard, shall I draw it?

Don Pedro   Dost thou wear thy wit by thy side?

Claudio   Never any did so, though very many have
been beside their wit. I will bid thee draw, as we do
the minstrels, draw to pleasure us.

Leonato   My lord, my lord—

Don Pedro   I will not listen to you.

Leonato   No? Come, brother; let's go! I will be heard.

Antonio   And you shall be heard or the two of you will suffer because of it.

[Leonato and Antonio exit.]

Don Pedro   See, see; here comes the man we went to find.

[Enter **Benedick**.]

Claudio   Now, Signior, what's the news?

Benedick   Good day, my lord.

Don Pedro   Welcome, Signior, you almost had to separate a fight.

Claudio   We just about had our two noses snapped off by two old men without teeth.

Don Pedro   Leonato and his brother. What do you think? If we had fought, I suspect that we would have been too young for them.

Benedick   In an unfair fight there is no true heroism. I came to find you both.

Claudio   We have been up and down looking for you because we are downhearted and would gladly have it chased away. Will you use your wit to help?

Benedick   It is in my scabbard. Shall I pull it out?

Don Pedro   Are you wearing your humor on your side?

Claudio   No one carries their wit on their side, although some have been beside their wit. Please, draw your wit as the musicians draw their bows. Make us happy.

Don Pedro   As I am an honest man, he looks pale.
131   Art thou sick, or angry?

Claudio   What, courage, man! What though care
kill'd a cat, thou hast mettle enough in thee to kill
care.

Benedick   Sir, I shall meet your wit in the career, and
you charge it against me. I pray you choose another
137   subject.

Claudio   Nay then give him another staff, this last
was broke cross.

Don Pedro   By this light, he changes more and
more. I think he be angry indeed.

Claudio   If he be, he knows how to turn his girdle.

Benedick   Shall I speak a word in your ear?

144   **Claudio**   God bless me from a challenge!

Benedick   [*Aside to Claudio.*] You are a villain. I jest
not; I will make it good how you dare, with what you
dare, and when you dare. Do me right; or I will protest your cowardice. You have kill'd a sweet lady,
and her death shall fall heavy on you. Let me hear
150   from you.

Claudio   Well, I will meet you, so I may have good
cheer.

Don Pedro   What, a feast, a feast?

Claudio   I' faith, I thank him, he hath bid me to a
calve's-head and a capon, the which if I do not carve
most curiously, say my knife's naught. Shall I not
157   find a woodcock too?

Benedick   Sir, your wit ambles well, it goes easily.

Don Pedro   Honestly, he looks pale. Are you sick or angry?

Claudio   Come on, step up, man! Care may have killed the cat, but you are strong enough to kill care.

Benedick   Sir, I will meet your wit at full speed if you use it as a weapon against me. Choose another person to attack.

Claudio   Give him another spear; this last one broke in half.

Don Pedro   By looking at him, he seems to be growing more and more pale. I think he really is angry.

Claudio   If he is, he knows what to do about it.

Benedick   Can I speak with you privately?

Claudio   God forbid, he wants to challenge me!

Benedick   [*aside to Claudio*] You are a villain; I am not kidding. I will prove my accusation however and with whatever you choose, and when you choose. Give me the satisfaction or I will announce your cowardice. You have killed a sweet lady and her death will fall heavy on your conscience. What do you say?

Claudio   Well, I will duel with you so that I can be entertained.

Don Pedro   What, are we having a feast?

Claudio   I thank him. He has invited me to carve a calf's head and a capon, and if I do not carve exquisitely, then I can say my knife is worthless. Will there be a woodcock too?

Benedick   Sir, you have a slow wit that wanders off easily.

Don Pedro   I'll tell thee how Beatrice prais'd thy
160   wit the other day. I said thou hadst a fine wit.
"True," said she, "a fine little one." "No," said I,
"a great wit." "Right," says she, "a great gross
one." "Nay," said I, "a good wit." "Just," said
she, "it hurts nobody." "Nay," said I, "the gentle-
165   man is wise." "Certain," said she, "a wise
gentleman." "Nay," said I, "he hath the tongues."
"That I believe," said she, "for he swore a thing to
me on Monday night, which he forswore on Tuesday
morning. There's a double tongue, there's two
170   tongues." Thus did she an hour together trans-
shape thy particular virtues, yet at last she con-
cluded with a sigh, thou wast the proper'st man in
Italy.

Claudio   For the which she wept heartily and said
175   she car'd not.

Don Pedro   Yea, that she did, but yet for all that,
and if she did not hate him deadly, she would love
him dearly. The old man's daughter told us all.

Claudio   All, all, and, moreover, God saw him
180   when he was hid in the garden.

Don Pedro   But when shall we set the savage bull's
horns on the sensible Benedick's head?

Claudio   Yea, and text underneath, "Here dwells
184   Benedick the married man"?

Don Pedro   Let me tell you how Beatrice praised your wit the other day. I said that you had a fine wit. "True," she said, "he has a fine little wit." "No," I said, you have "a great wit." "Right," she says, "a huge and ugly one." Of course I say, "a good wit." "It's a just wit," she said, "it doesn't hurt anybody." "No," I said, "the gentleman is wise." "Of course," she said, "a wise gentleman." "No," I said, "he can speak many languages." "That I can believe," said she, "because he swore one thing to me on Monday night, and took it back on Tuesday morning; there's a double tongue, there's two languages." During an hour together she altered all your assets, but at last she came to the conclusion, with a sigh, that you were the finest man in Italy.

Claudio   With that she cried excessively and said she didn't care.

Don Pedro   Yes, she did that. But yet after all that, she said that if she didn't hate him to death, she would love him too much. The old man's daughter told us everything.

Claudio   Everything, everything, and furthermore, God saw Benedick when he was hiding in the garden.

Don Pedro   But when will we see Benedick a married man?

Claudio   Yes, and with a sign underneath him that reads, "Here dwells Benedick, the married man?"

Benedick   Fare you well, boy, you know my mind. I
will leave you now to your gossip-like humor. You
break jests as braggards do their blades, which God
be thank'd, hurt not. My lord, for your many
courtesies I thank you. I must discontinue your com-
190   pany. Your brother the bastard is fled from
Messina. You have among you kill'd a sweet and
innocent lady. For my Lord Lack-beard there, he
and I shall meet, and till then peace be with him.

[*Exit.*]

194   **Don Pedro**   He is in earnest.

Claudio   In most profound earnest, and I'll warrant you, for the love of Beatrice.

Don Pedro   And hath challeng'd thee?

198   **Claudio**   Most sincerely.

Don Pedro   What a pretty thing man is when he
goes in his doublet and hose and leaves off his wit!

Enter Constables [**Dogberry** *and* **Verges**, *and the* **Watch**
with] **Conrade** *and* **Borachio**.

Claudio   He is then a giant to an ape, but then is
202   an ape a doctor to such a man.

Don Pedro   But soft you, let me be. Pluck up, my
heart, and be sad. Did he not say my brother was
205   fled?

Dogberry   Come you, sir. If justice cannot tame you,
she shall ne'er weigh more reasons in her balance.
Nay, and you be a cursing hypocrite once, you must
209   be look'd to.

Don Pedro   How now? two of my brother's men
bound? Borachio one!

Benedick   Good-bye, boy, you know what my intentions
are. I will leave you now to your gossiping mood. You make
jokes as braggarts break their blades, which, thank God,
don't hurt. My lord, for your many kindnesses, I thank you,
but I must leave your court. Your brother the bastard has fled
from Messina, and you have among the three of you killed a
sweet and innocent lady. But as for my Lord Lackbeard there,
he and I will meet. Until then, peace be with him.

[*Benedick exits.*]

Don Pedro   He is serious.

Claudio   Extremely serious, and I promise you that it is for
the love of Beatrice.

Don Pedro   And he has challenged you.

Claudio   Yes, he has, most sincerely.

Don Pedro   What a pretty thing man is when he wears his
fancy clothes and forgets to wear his intelligence.

[*Enter* **Dogberry**, **Verges**, *and the* **Watch**, *with* **Conrade**
and **Borachio**.]

Claudio   He is bigger in the eyes of an ape; but then an ape
is a doctor to such a man because he is smarter.

Don Pedro   Listen, let me take courage to heart and be
serious. Didn't he say that my brother has fled?

Dogberry   Come here, you; if justice is not served she will
never be able to weigh more reasons in her balance—
because you are a cursing hypocrite and we have to look
after you.

Don Pedro   What's going on? Two of my brother's men tied
up! Borachio for one!

Claudio   Hearken after their offense, my lord.

Don Pedro   Officers, what offense have these men
214   done?

Dogberry   Marry, sir, they have committed false report; moreover they have spoken untruths; secondarily, they are slanders; sixt and lastly, they
have belied a lady; thirdly, they have verified unjust things; and to conclude, they are lying knaves.

220 **Don Pedro**   First, I ask thee what they have
done; thirdly, I ask thee what's their offense; sixt
and lastly, why they are committed; and to conclude,
what you lay to their charge.

Claudio   Rightly reason'd, and in his own division,
225   and by my troth there's one meaning well suited.

Don Pedro   Who have you offended, masters,
that you are thus bound to your answer? This
learned constable is too cunning to be understood.
229   What's your offense?

Borachio   Sweet Prince, let me go no farther to mine
answer: do you hear me, and let this count kill me.
I have deceiv'd even your very eyes. What your wisdoms could not discover, these shallow fools have
brought to light, who in the night overheard me
235   confessing to this man how Don John your
brother incens'd me to slander the Lady Hero,
how you were brought into the orchard, and saw me
court Margaret in Hero's garments, how you dis-
grac'd her when you should marry her. My villainy
240   they have upon record, which I had rather seal
with my death than repeat over to my shame. The
lady is dead upon mine and my master's false accusation; and briefly, I desire nothing but the reward of
a villain.

Claudio   Ask them what they have done, my lord.

Don Pedro   Officers, what offense have these men committed?

Dogberry   Well, sir, they have made a false report; moreover, they have lied; secondarily, they are liars; sixth and lastly, they have lied about a lady; thirdly they have verified unjust things; and in conclusion, they are lying rascals.

Don Pedro   First, let me ask you what they have done; thirdly, I ask you what's their offense; sixth and lastly, why are they arrested; and, to conclude, what charges do you lay at them?

Claudio   Well done and in a way only he would understand. And in truth, he was able to say the same thing many different ways.

Don Pedro   What have you done to be bound in such a way? This learned constable is too clever to be understood. What did you do?

Borachio   Sweet Prince, don't let me go any farther to answer, listen to me and then let this count kill me. I have deceived your eyes, and what your wisdoms could not discover, these fools have brought to light. They overheard me telling this man how your brother Don John incited me to slander Lady Hero. You were brought into the orchard and you saw me court Margaret in Hero's clothes. You have disgraced her, when you should have married her. The record of my crime is true, and I would rather guarantee it with my death than repeat my shame. The lady is dead upon mine and my master's false accusations. I desire nothing but the reward of a criminal.

Don Pedro   Runs not this speech like iron through
245   your blood?

Claudio   I have drunk poison whiles he utter'd it.

Don Pedro   But did my brother set thee on to this?

Borachio   Yea, and paid me richly for the practice of it.

Don Pedro   He is compos'd and fram'd of treachery,
250   and fled he is upon this villainy.

Claudio   Sweet Hero, now thy image doth appear
in the rare semblance that I lov'd it first.

Dogberry   Come, bring away the plaintiffs. By this
time our sexton hath reform'd Signior Leonato of
255   the matter; and, masters, do not forget to specify,
when time and place shall serve, that I am an ass.

Verges   Here, here comes Master Signior Leonato,
and the Sexton too.

*Enter **Leonato**, his brother [**Antonio**], and the **Sexton**.*

Leonato   Which is the villain? Let me see his eyes,
260   That when I note another man like him
I may avoid him. Which of these is he?

Borachio   If you would know your wronger, look on me.

Leonato   Art thou the slave that with thy breath hast kill'd
Mine innocent child?

Borachio   Yea, even I alone.

265 **Leonato**   No, not so, villain, thou beliest thyself.
Here stand a pair of honorable men,
A third is fled, that had a hand in it.
I thank you, princes, for my daughter's death;
Record it with your high and worthy deeds.
270   'Twas bravely done, if you bethink you of it.

Don Pedro Doesn't this speech make your blood run cold like iron?

Claudio I have drunk poison while he told it.

Don Pedro But did my brother put you up to this?

Borachio Yes, and he paid me well for putting it into play.

Don Pedro He is built and created from treachery, and he has escaped as a result of this villainy.

Claudio Sweet Hero! Now your image appears in the rare form of that when I first loved it.

Dogberry Come, bring the plaintiffs [*he means "defendants"*]. By now our sexton has reformed [*he means to say "informed"*] Signior Leonato of the matter, and, gentlemen, do not forget to state when it is convenient, that I am an ass.

Verges Here comes Master Signior Leonato, and the sexton too.

[*Re-enter* **Leonato** *and* **Antonio**, *with the* **Sexton**.]

Leonato Who is the villain? Let me see his eyes so that when I see another man that looks like him, I can avoid him. Which of these is he?

Borachio If you want to know your deceiver, look at me.

Leonato Are you the slave that killed my innocent child with your slanderous words?

Borachio Yes, I alone.

Leonato No, that's not true, villain. You're lying to yourself because here is a pair of honorable men; the third has fled who also helped you. I thank you, princes, for my daughter's death. Make note of it on your list of noble and worthy deeds. It was bravely done if you think of it.

Claudio   I know not how to pray your patience,
Yet I must speak. Choose your revenge yourself,
Impose me to what penance your invention
Can lay upon my sin; yet sinn'd I not,
But in mistaking.

275 **Don Pedro**   By my soul, nor I,
And yet, to satisfy this good old man,
I would bend under any heavy weight
That he'll enjoin me to.

Leonato   I cannot bid you bid my daughter live—
280   That were impossible—but I pray you both,
Possess the people in Messina here
How innocent she died, and if your love
Can labor aught in sad invention,
Hang her an epitaph upon her tomb,
285   And sing it to her bones, sing it to-night.
To-morrow morning come you to my house,
And since you could not be my son-in-law,
Be yet my nephew. My brother hath a daughter,
Almost the copy of my child that's dead,
290   And she alone is heir to both of us.
Give her the right you should have giv'n her cousin,
And so dies my revenge.

Claudio   O noble sir,
Your overkindness doth wring tears from me.
I do embrace your offer, and dispose
295   For henceforth of poor Claudio.

Leonato   To-morrow then I will expect your coming,
To-night I take my leave. This naughty man
Shall face to face be brought to Margaret,
299   Who I believe was pack'd in all this wrong,
Hir'd to it by your brother.

210

Claudio   I do not know how to beg for your patience, but I have to say something. Choose your revenge and impose any punishment that you can think of for my sins, but even though I have sinned, it was a mistake.

Don Pedro   From my soul, me too. To appease this good old man I would endure any punishment that he would command.

Leonato   I cannot ask you to allow my daughter to live, that is impossible. But I beg you both to explain to the people in Messina that she was innocent when she died. If your love can construct something from its sadness then hang an epitaph for her on her tomb and sing it to her bones tonight. Tomorrow morning, come to my house and, though you could not be my son-in-law, you can be my nephew. My brother has a daughter who looks almost the same as my child who is dead. She is the only heir to the both of us; give to her what you should have given her cousin. And with that, my revenge will die.

Claudio   Oh noble sir, your extreme kindness brings tears to my eyes. I will accept your offer with open arms and from now on, I am at your disposal.

Leonato   Tomorrow then I will expect your arrival, and now I will leave. This naughty man will have to face Margaret, who I believe was an accomplice to all of this wrong and hired by your brother.

Borachio   No, by my soul she was not,
Nor knew not what she did when she spoke to me,
But always hath been just and virtuous
303 In any thing that I do know by her.

Dogberry   Moreover, sir, which indeed is not under
white and black, this plaintiff here, the offender,
did call me ass. I beseech you let it be remem-
b'red in his punishment. And also, the watch heard
them talk of one Deformed. They say he wears a key
309 in his ear and a lock hanging by it, and borrows
money in God's name, the which he hath us'd
so long and never paid that now men grow hard-hearted
and will lend nothing for God's sake. Pray you
313 examine him upon that point.

Leonato   I thank thee for thy care and honest pains.

Dogberry   Your worship speaks like a most thankful
and reverent youth, and I praise God for you.

Leonato   There's for thy pains.

Dogberry   God save the foundation!

Leonato   Go, I discharge thee of thy prisoner, and I
320 thank thee.

Dogberry   I leave an arrant knave with your worship,
which I beseech your worship to correct yourself, for
the example of others. God keep your worship! I
wish your worship well. God restore you to health! I
325 I humbly give you leave to depart, and if a merry
meeting may be wish'd, God prohibit it! Come,
neighbor.

[*Exeunt Dogberry and Verges.*]

212

Borachio No, by my soul, she was not involved and did not know what she did when she was speaking to me. She has always been fair and honorable in everything that I know of her.

Dogberry Moreover, sir, this is not written down in white and black, but this plaintiff [*he means "defendant"*], the offender, did call me an ass. I beg you let it be remembered in his punishment. And also, the watch heard them talk of someone named Deformed; they say he wears a key in his ear with a lock hanging from it. He borrows money from people in the name of God and never pays it back. And now, people have grown hard-hearted and will not lend anything in God's name. Please, ask him about that.

Leonato I thank you for your care and honest efforts.

Dogberry You speak like a thankful and respectful boy, and may God bless you.

Leonato [*giving Dogberry some money*] This is for your efforts.

Dogberry God save the foundation [*he means "God bless the founder"*]!

Leonato Go, I will take your prisoner from you, and I thank you again.

Dogberry I leave a complete rascal with you, who beg you to punish and to make an example of for others. God bless you. I wish you well. God restore your health! I will humbly leave and if we should meet in the future, may God prohibit [*he means "permit"*] it! Come, neighbor.

[*Dogberry and Verges exit.*]

213

Leonato   Until to-morrow morning, lords, farewell.

Antonio   Farewell, my lords, we look for you to-morrow.

Don Pedro   We will not fail.

Claudio   To-night I'll mourn with Hero.

Leonato   [*To the Watch.*] Bring you these fellows on.—
331   We'll talk with Margaret,
        How her acquaintance grew with this lewd fellow.

Exeunt [*severally*].

Scene 2

Enter **Benedick** *and* **Margaret**, [*meeting*].

Benedick   Pray thee, sweet Mistress Margaret, de-
    serve well at my hands by helping me to the speech
    of Beatrice.

Margaret   Will you then write me a sonnet in praise
5   of my beauty?

Benedick   In so high a style, Margaret, that no man
    living shall come over it, for in most comely truth
    thou deservest it.

Margaret   To have no man come over me? Why,
10   shall I always keep below stairs?

Benedick   Thy wit is as quick as the greyhound's
    mouth, it catches.

Margaret   And yours as blunt as the fencer's foils,
14   which hit, but hurt not.

Leonato   Until tomorrow morning, lords, good-bye.

Antonio   Good-bye, my lords, we will look for you tomorrow.

Don Pedro   We will be there.

Claudio   Tonight I'll mourn Hero.

Leonato   [*to the Watch*] Bring these fellows along. We'll talk with Margaret and learn how she became acquainted with this vulgar fellow.

[*They all exit.*]

Scene 2

Enter **Benedick** *and* **Margaret**, *meeting in Leonato's garden.*

Benedick   Please, sweet Miss Margaret, give me a hand and help me write a poem about Beatrice.

Margaret   Will you write a sonnet praising my beauty afterwards?

Benedick   I'll write a poem in such an elegant style, Margaret, that no man living could come over [*exceed*] it, and truthfully, you deserve it.

Margaret   No man come over me! Will I always be kept downstairs in the servants' quarters?

Benedick   Your wit is as quick as the greyhound's mouth—it catches everything it chases.

Margaret   And yours as blunt as the fencer's sword with a dull tip—they hit, but don't hurt anyone.

Benedick   A most manly wit, Margaret, it will not
hurt a woman. And so I pray thee call Beatrice;
I give thee the bucklers.

Margaret   Give us the swords, we have bucklers of
19   our own.

Benedick   If you use them, Margaret, you must put
in the pikes with a vice, and they are dangerous
weapons for maids.

Margaret   Well, I will call Beatrice to you, who I
think hath legs.

Exit Margaret.

25   **Benedick**   And therefore will come.

[*Sings.*]

"The god of love,
   That sits above,
And knows me, and knows me,
29   How pitiful I deserve"—

I mean in singing; but in loving, Leander the good
swimmer, Troilus the first employer of pandars,
and a whole bookful of these quondam carpet-
mongers, whose names yet run smoothly in the
even road of a blank verse, why, they were never
35   so truly turn'd over and over as my poor self in
love. Marry, I cannot show it in rhyme; I have tried.
I can find out no rhyme to "lady" but "baby," an
innocent rhyme; for "scorn," "horn," a hard rhyme;
for "school," "fool," a babbling rhyme: very ominous
endings. No, I was not born under a rhyming planet,
41   nor I cannot woo in festival terms.

Enter **Beatrice**.

Sweet Beatrice, wouldst thou come when I call'd thee?

Benedick   It is a gentlemanly wit, Margaret, not intended to hurt a woman. Please go get Beatrice; I give up on this duel of wits.

Margaret   Give us women the swords, we have our own shields.

Benedick   If you use them, Margaret, you must add spikes with a vice and know that they are dangerous weapons for virgins.

Margaret   Well, I'll call Beatrice for you, but she can get here on her own—she has legs.

[*Margaret exits.*]

Benedick   And that means that she will come.

[*Benedick sings.*]

The god of love,
That sits above,
And knows me, and knows me,
How pitiful I deserve,—

I am horrible at singing, but in loving, that's something else. Leander and Troilus or an entire book full of these legendary lover types whose names sound so smooth in a line of blank verse, not one of them has been as completely captivated or as anxiously in love as I am. Certainly, I cannot show my love in a rhyme, I have tried. The only rhyming word that I can find for "lady" is "baby," which is childish; the only word I can find to rhyme with "scorn" is "horn" and that is a harsh-sounding rhyme; and the only word that I can find that rhymes with "school" is "fool," which is an absurd rhyme. They all have ill-conceived endings. No, I was not born to be a poet nor can I woo a lady with joyful words.

[*Enter* **Beatrice**.]

Sweet Beatrice, did you come because I called you?

Beatrice   Yea, signior, and depart when you bid me.

45 **Benedick**   O, stay but till then!

Beatrice   "Then" is spoken; fare you well now.
And yet ere I go, let me go with that I came, which
is, with knowing what hath pass'd between you
and Claudio.

Benedick   Only foul words—and thereupon I will
51 kiss thee.

Beatrice   Foul words is but foul wind, and foul wind
is but foul breath, and foul breath is noisome; therefore
54 I will depart unkiss'd.

Benedick   Thou hast frighted the word out of his
right sense, so forcible is thy wit. But I must tell
thee plainly, Claudio undergoes my challenge, and
either I must shortly hear from him, or I will sub-
scribe him a coward. And I pray thee now tell me,
for which of my bad parts didst thou first fall in love
61 with me?

Beatrice   For them all together, which maintain'd
so politic a state of evil that they will not admit any
good part to intermingle with them. But for which
65 of my good parts did you first suffer love for me?

Benedick   Suffer love! a good epithite! I do suffer
love indeed, for I love thee against my will.

Beatrice   In spite of your heart, I think. Alas, poor
heart, if you spite it for my sake, I will spite it for
yours, for I will never love that which my friend
71 hates.

Benedick   Thou and I are too wise to woo peaceably.

Beatrice   Yes, Signior, and I will leave when you ask me to.

Benedick   Oh, well, stay until then!

Beatrice   Since you just said "then" I will leave you now, but before I go, let me ask you what I came to find out, which is to know what happened between you and Claudio.

Benedick   I spoke only foul words to him, and with that I will kiss you.

Beatrice   If you had foul words in your mouth, you must have foul breath, and foul breath is foul-smelling; and with that, I will leave without being kissed.

Benedick   With your strong wit, you frightened the meanings right out of your words. But, I will tell you simply that I have challenged Claudio, and he must either accept the challenge soon or I'll write him down as a coward. And now, please tell me, which of my bad traits did you fall in love with first?

Beatrice   All of them together, because they are so well maintained in a state of evilness that it would be impossible to allow any good traits to mix with them. But, from which of my good traits did you first suffer the pains of love?

Benedick   Suffer love! That's a good expression. Of course I do suffer love, because I love you against my will.

Beatrice   You love me in spite of your heart I think—oh, poor heart! If you spite your heart for my sake, then I will spite my heart for yours, because I will never love something that my friend hates.

Benedick   You and I are too clever to woo peaceably.

Beatrice   It appears not in this confession; there's
not one wise man among twenty that will praise
75   himself.

Benedick   An old, an old instance, Beatrice, that
liv'd in the time of good neighbors. If a man do
not erect in this age his own tomb ere he dies, he
shall live no longer in monument than the bell rings
80   and the widow weeps.

Beatrice   And how long is that, think you?

Benedick   Question: why, an hour in clamor and
83   a quarter in rheum; therefore is it most expedient
for the wise, if Don Worm (his conscience) find no
impediment to the contrary, to be the trumpet of
his own virtues, as I am to myself. So much for
praising myself, who I myself will bear witness is
praiseworthy. And now tell me, how doth your
89   cousin?

Beatrice   Very ill.

Benedick   And how do you?

Beatrice   Very ill too.

Benedick   Serve God, love me, and mend. There
94   will I leave you too, for here comes one in haste.

Enter **Ursula**.

Ursula   Madam, you must come to your uncle,
yonder's old coil at home. It is prov'd my Lady
Hero hath been falsely accus'd, the Prince and
98   Claudio mightily abus'd, and Don John is the
author of all, who is fled and gone. Will you come
presently?

Beatrice   Not a single wise man in twenty will praise himself, but from what you just said, you are not wise.

Benedick   That's an old saying, Beatrice, from a time when neighbors spoke kindly of one another. As it is now, if a man doesn't build his own tomb before he dies, he will not be remembered longer than the bells ringing and the widows weeping.

Beatrice   And how long is that, do you think?

Benedick   That's a good question—probably an hour for the bell ringing and about a quarter of an hour for the weeping. Because of that, it is practical if a man's conscience and the worms that gnaw in it avoid obstacles to the contrary and proclaim his own virtues as I do and, with me as my witness, find quite praiseworthy. But now, tell me, how is your cousin?

Beatrice   She is very ill.

Benedick   And how are you?

Beatrice   Very ill as well.

Benedick   Praise God, love me and get better—and that's where I'll leave you too, because here comes someone in a hurry.

[*Enter* **Ursula**.]

Ursula   Madam, you must go see your uncle. There's all kinds of turmoil at home. It has been proven that my Lady Hero has been accused falsely. The Prince and Claudio have been greatly deceived, and Don John, the cause all of these troubles, has up and left. Will you come now?

Beatrice   Will you go hear this news, signior?

Benedick   I will live in thy heart, die in thy lap, and be
buried in thy eyes; and moreover I will go with thee to
104   thy uncle's.

Exeunt.

Scene 3

Enter **Claudio**, *Prince* [**Don Pedro**], *and three or four
with tapers.*

Claudio   Is this the monument of Leonato?

[A] Lord   It is, my lord.

[*Claudio reading out of a scroll.*]

EPITAPH

"Done to death by slanderous tongues
Was the Hero that here lies.
5   Death, in guerdon of her wrongs,
Gives her fame which never dies.
So the life that died with shame
Lives in death with glorious fame."

Hang thou there upon the tomb,

[*Hangs up the scroll.*]

10   Praising her when I am [dumb].
Now, music, sound, and sing your solemn hymn.

Beatrice   Will you go with me to hear this news, Signior?

Benedick   I will live in your heart, die in your lap, and be buried in your eyes, and with that I will go with you to your uncle's.

[*They exit.*]

Scene 3

Enter **Don Pedro**, **Claudio**, *and three or four others with candles in a church yard.*

Claudio   Is this the tomb of Leonato's family?

Lord   Yes, it is, my lord.

Claudio   [*reading out of a scroll*]

Dead because of slanderous words,
It is here that Hero lies.
Death, in repayment for being wronged,
Gives her fame, which never dies.
So the life that died with shame
Lives in death with celebrated fame.

[*He hangs the scroll on the tomb.*]

This epitaph will hang upon the tomb praising her long after I am dead. Now, play the music and sing your solemn hymn.

SONG.

Pardon, goddess of the night,
Those that slew thy virgin knight,
For the which, with songs of woe,
15   Round about her tomb they go.
      Midnight, assist our moan,
      Help us to sigh and groan,
          Heavily, heavily.
      Graves, yawn and yield your dead,
20   Till death be uttered,
          Heavily, heavily.

[*Claudio*]

Now, unto thy bones good night!
Yearly will I do this rite.

Don Pedro   Good morrow, masters, put your torches out.
25   The wolves have preyed, and look, the gentle day,
Before the wheels of Phoebus, round about
Dapples the drowsy east with spots of grey.
Thanks to you all, and leave us. Fare you well.

Claudio   Good morrow, masters—each his several way.

30 **Don Pedro**   Come let us hence, and put on other weeds,
And then to Leonato's we will go.

Claudio   And Hymen now with luckier issue speed's
Than this for whom we rend'red up this woe.

Exeunt.

[*Singing.*]

Pardon, goddess of the night,
Those that slew your virgin knight;
These men sing songs of woe,
Around her tomb they go.
Midnight, help our moans;
Help us to sigh and groan,
Heavily, heavily:
Graves, open and release your dead,
Until death is fully expressed,
Heavily, heavily.

Claudio   For now I will say good-night to your bones, but I
will perform this ceremony every year.

Don Pedro   Good morning, sirs; put out your torches. The
wolves have finished hunting, and look, the gentle dawn
has arrived; before the sun fully illuminates, it mottles the
drowsy eastern sky with spots of grey. Thanks to all of you,
you may go, good-bye.

Claudio   Good morning, gentlemen, we will go our separate
ways.

Don Pedro   Come on, let's get going. We'll change our
clothes and then go to Leonato's.

Claudio   And hopefully, the god of love will favor us with
better results than for Hero, for whom we caused this
sadness.

[*They exit.*]

Scene 4

Enter **Leonato, Benedick, [Beatrice,] Margaret, Ursula,**
old man **[Antonio], Friar [Francis], Hero.**

Friar   Did I not tell you she was innocent?

Leonato   So are the Prince and Claudio, who accus'd her
Upon the error that you heard debated.
But Margaret was in some fault for this,
5   Although against her will, as it appears
In the true course of all the question.

Antonio   Well, I am glad that all things sort so well.

Benedick   And so am I, being else by faith enforc'd
9   To call young Claudio to a reckoning for it.

Leonato   Well, daughter, and you gentlewomen all,
Withdraw into a chamber by yourselves,
And when I send for you, come hither masked.
The Prince and Claudio promis'd by this hour
To visit me. You know your office, brother:
15   You must be father to your brother's daughter,
And give her to young Claudio.

Exeunt Ladies.

Antonio   Which I will do with confirm'd countenance.

Benedick   Friar, I must entreat your pains, I think.

Friar   To do what, signior?

20 **Benedick**   To bind me, or undo me—one of them.
Signior Leonato, truth it is, good signior,
Your niece regards me with an eye of favor.

Scene 4

Enter **Leonato, Antonio, Benedick, Beatrice, Margaret, Ursula, Friar Francis,** *and* **Hero** *in a room in Leonato's house.*

Friar Francis   Didn't I tell you that she was innocent?

Leonato   The Prince and Claudio who accused her erroneously are innocent too, because they were deceived as you have heard discussed. But Margaret is guilty in part for this, although after an investigation, her participation was not deliberate.

Antonio   Well, I am glad that everything has been sorted out so well.

Benedick   And so am I, otherwise I would have been forced to keep my promise and make Claudio account for his behavior.

Leonato   Well, daughter, and all of you ladies, isolate yourselves in a room and when I send for you, come here with your masks.

[*The ladies exit.*]

The Prince and Claudio promised to be here with me by now. Brother, you know your job: to be a father to your niece and give her in marriage to young Claudio.

Antonio   Which I will do with a serious expression on my face.

Benedick   Friar, I must ask for your help, I think.

Friar Francis   To do what, Signior?

Benedick   Well, to tie me up, or to destroy me, one of the two. Signior Leonato, the truth is, good Signior, your niece is quite fond of me.

227

Leonato   That eye my daughter lent her, 'tis most true.

Benedick   And I do with an eye of love requite her.

25 **Leonato**   The sight whereof I think you had from me,
From Claudio, and the Prince. But what's your will?

Benedick   Your answer, sir, is enigmatical,
But for my will, my will is your good will
May stand with ours, this day to be conjoin'd
30   In the state of honorable marriage,
In which, good friar, I shall desire your help.

Leonato   My heart is with your liking.

Friar   And my help.
Here comes the Prince and Claudio.

Enter Prince [**Don Pedro**] *and* **Claudio** *and two or
three other.*

Don Pedro   Good morrow to this fair assembly.

35 **Leonato**   Good morrow, Prince; good morrow, Claudio;
We here attend you. Are you yet determined
To-day to marry with my brother's daughter?

Claudio   I'll hold my mind were she an Ethiope.

Leonato   Call her forth, brother, here's the friar ready.

                                    [*Exit Antonio.*]

40 **Don Pedro**   Good morrow, Benedick. Why, what's the matter,
That you have such a February face,
So full of frost, of storm, and cloudiness?

Leonato   She sees through the same eyes of love as my daughter, that is very true.

Benedick   And with the same eyes of love, I return her feelings.

Leonato   I believe your vision was enhanced by me, Claudio, and the Prince, but what do you want?

Benedick   Your answer, sir, is perplexing, but as for what I want, I want your best wishes and blessings to be united in an honorable marriage, in which, good Friar, I will need your help.

Leonato   My blessings are as you would like.

Friar Francis   And my help as well. Here come the Prince and Claudio.

[**Don Pedro** and **Claudio** and two or three others enter.]

Don Pedro   Good morning to all of you.

Leonato   Good morning, Prince, good morning, Claudio. We were waiting for you. Are you still determined to marry my brother's daughter today?

Claudio   I would not change my mind if she were an Ethiopian with dark skin.

Leonato   Brother, ask her to come out, the Friar is ready.

[Antonio exits.]

Don Pedro   Good morning, Benedick. What's the matter? Your face looks like the month of February, all full of frost, storms, and clouds.

Claudio   I think he thinks upon the savage bull.
Tush, fear not, man, we'll tip thy horns with gold,
45   And all Europa shall rejoice at thee,
As once Europa did at lusty Jove,
When he would play the noble beast in love.

Benedick   Bull Jove, sir, had an amiable low,
And some such strange bull leapt your father's cow,
50   And got a calf in that same noble feat
Much like to you, for you have just his bleat.

Enter Brother [**Antonio**], **Hero**, **Beatrice**, **Margaret**,
Ursula, [*the ladies masked*].

Claudio   For this I owe you: here comes other reck'nings.
Which is the lady I must seize upon?

Antonio   This same is she, and I do give you her.

55 **Claudio**   Why then she's mine. Sweet, let me see your face.

Leonato   No, that you shall not till you take her hand,
Before this friar, and swear to marry her.

Claudio   Give me your hand before this holy friar—
59   I am your husband if you like of me.

Hero   [*Unmasking.*] And when I liv'd, I was your other wife,
And when you lov'd, you were my other husband.

Claudio   Another Hero!

Hero   Nothing certainer:
One Hero died defil'd, but I do live,
64   And surely as I live, I am a maid.

Don Pedro   The former Hero! Hero that is dead!

Leonato   She died, my lord, but whiles her slander liv'd.

Claudio   I think he is thinking about the savage bull that is about to become tamed. Hey, don't be afraid, we will dress you up by tipping your horns with gold and all of Europe will express joy with you, just like Europa [*daughter of a Phoenician king*] did with the lively Jove [*Roman god of the sky*] when he turned himself into a bull in love.

Benedick   Jove the bull, sir, bellowed for love. And a similar strange bull mated with your father's cow and had a calf in the same way, just like you, for you have his moan.

Claudio   I'll pay you back for that, but here come other matters to be dealt with.

[**Antonio** *re-enters with the ladies wearing masks*]

Which is the lady that I am supposed to take hold of?

Antonio   This is she, and I do give her to you.

Claudio   So, then she is mine. Sweet lady, can I see your face?

Leonato   No, you cannot see her until you take her hand and, in front of this friar, promise to marry her.

Claudio   Give me your hand and before this holy friar, if you want me, I am your husband.

Hero   And when I lived, I was your other wife [*unmasking*], and when you loved, you were my other husband.

Claudio   Another Hero!

Hero   Nothing more certain. One Hero died dishonored, but I do live, and as surely as I live, I am a virgin.

Don Pedro   Another Hero! Just like the Hero that is dead!

Leonato   She was dead, my lord, only as long as her slander was alive.

Friar   All this amazement can I qualify,
When after that the holy rites are ended,
I'll tell you largely of fair Hero's death:
70 Mean time let wonder seem familiar,
And to the chapel let us presently.

Benedick   Soft and fair, friar. Which is Beatrice?

Beatrice   [*Unmasking.*] I answer to that name. What
is your will?

Benedick   Do not you love me?

Beatrice   Why, no, no more than reason.

75 **Benedick**   Why then your uncle and the Prince and Claudio
Have been deceived. They swore you did.

Beatrice   Do not you love me?

Benedick   Troth, no, no more than reason.

Beatrice   Why then my cousin, Margaret, and Ursula
Are much deceiv'd, for they did swear you did.

80 **Benedick**   They swore that you were almost sick for me.

Beatrice   They swore that you were well-nigh dead for me.

Benedick   'Tis no such matter. Then you do not love me?

Beatrice   No, truly, but in friendly recompense.

Leonato   Come, cousin, I am sure you love the gentleman.

Claudio   And I'll be sworn upon't that he loves her,
86 For here's a paper written in his hand,
A halting sonnet of his own pure brain,
Fashion'd to Beatrice.

Friar Francis   All this is shocking, and I will explain everything after the holy rites are finished. I will tell you about fair Hero's death. In the meantime, accept these miraculous events as though they were everyday occurrences. Let's go to the chapel now.

Benedick   Wait a moment, friar. Which one is Beatrice?

Beatrice   [*unmasking*] I answer to that name. What would you like?

Benedick   Do you love me?

Beatrice   Why, no: no more than is reasonable.

Benedick   Well, then your uncle and the Prince and Claudio have been deceived; they swore that you loved me.

Beatrice   Do you love me?

Benedick   Honestly, no; no more than is reasonable.

Beatrice   Well, then my cousin, Margaret, and Ursula were greatly deceived because they swore that you did.

Benedick   They swore that you were almost lovesick for me.

Beatrice   They swore that you were nearly dead in love for me.

Benedick   Then it isn't true, you don't love me?

Beatrice   Truly, no, only in a friendly manner.

Leonato   Come on, cousin, I am sure you love the gentleman.

Claudio   And I'll swear that he loves her because here is a paper in his handwriting. [*holding up a piece of paper*] It is an awkward sonnet produced entirely from his brain and it is addressed to Beatrice.

Hero   And here's another
Writ in my cousin's hand, stol'n from her pocket,
90   Containing her affection unto Benedick.

Benedick   A miracle! here's our own hands against
our hearts. Come, I will have thee, but, by this light,
I take thee for pity.

Beatrice   I would not deny you, but by this good
95   day, I yield upon great persuasion, and partly
to save your life, for I was told you were in a con-
sumption.

Benedick   Peace, I will stop your mouth.

[*Kissing her.*]

99 **Don Pedro**   How dost thou, Benedick the married man?

Benedick   I'll tell thee what, Prince: a college of
wit-crackers cannot flout me out of my humor.
Dost thou think I care for a satire or an epigram?
No, if a man will be beaten with brains, 'a shall
104   wear nothing handsome about him. In brief,
since I do purpose to marry, I will think nothing to
any purpose that the world can say against it, and
therefore never flout at me for what I have said
against it; for man is a giddy thing, and this is my
109   conclusion. For thy part, Claudio, I did think
to have beaten thee, but in that thou art like to be
my kinsman, live unbruis'd, and love my cousin.

Claudio   I had well hop'd thou wouldst have denied
113   Beatrice, that I might have cudgell'd thee out
of thy single life, to make thee a double-dealer,
which out of question thou wilt be, if my cousin
do not look exceedingly narrowly to thee.

Hero   And here's another one written in my cousin's hand-writing and stolen from her pocket. It admits her affection for Benedick.

Benedick   A miracle! Our own handwritings confirm what our hearts feel. Come on, I will marry you, but only out of pity for you.

Beatrice   I wouldn't deny you, but I surrender under a great deal of persuasion and partly to save your life, because I was told you were lovesick and wasting away.

Benedick   Peace! I will stop your mouth with a kiss.

[*Kisses her.*]

Don Pedro   How do you feel being Benedick, the married man?

Benedick   I'll tell you what, Prince: An entire company of jokesters could not mock me out of my state of mind. Do you think I am bothered by name-calling? No. If a man is afraid of what he is called, there wouldn't be anything attractive about him. In short, since I do plan to marry, I won't care if anyone says something against it. Therefore, don't mock me for what I have said against it in the past, because man is a flighty thing and that is my answer. As for you, Claudio, although I know I would have beaten you in our duel, since you are about to become my kinsman, I will let you go without injuries to love my cousin.

Claudio   I was hoping you would have said no to Beatrice, and that way I could have clobbered you out of your unmarried life to make you an unfaithful husband, which without a doubt you will be if my cousin does not keep a close watch on you.

Benedick   Come, come, we are friends. Let's have a
dance ere we are married, that we may lighten our
own hearts and our wives' heels.

120 **Leonato**   We'll have dancing afterward.

Benedick   First, of my word; therefore play, music.
Prince, thou art sad, get thee a wife, get thee a wife.
There is no staff more reverent than one tipp'd with
horn.

Enter **Messenger**.

Messenger   My lord, your brother John is ta'en in flight,
126   And brought with armed men back to Messina.

Benedick   Think not on him till to-morrow. I'll
devise thee brave punishments for him. Strike up,
pipers.

Dance.

[*Exeunt.*]

Benedick   Come on, come on, we are friends; let's have a dance before we are married so that we can lighten our hearts and our wives' heels.

Leonato   We'll dance after the weddings.

Benedick   First, on my word! Let the music play. Prince, you are sad—get a wife, get a wife. Your royal staff would be far more worthy if it had a horned tip.

[*A* **Messenger** *enters.*]

Messenger   My lord, your brother John has been caught and is being brought back to Messina by armed men.

Benedick   Don't think about him until tomorrow. I'll help you invent some imposing punishments for him. Let the music play.

[*Dance*]

[*Everyone exits.*]

Activities

Characters

The answers to the following questions can be found by searching the **original** text. These questions should help you become more familiar with the characters' personalities.

Leonato

1 The reader is introduced to Leonato in the first line of the play. What is Leonato's first question to the messenger? Does this say anything about his personality?

2 Leonato also asks the messenger if Claudio's uncle broke out into tears when he heard the good news about his nephew. What is the response to his question?

3 Describe the relationship between Leonato and his daughter Hero in the early parts of the play.

4 How does Leonato welcome Don John? Does he treat him any differently?

5 Who is Leonato's brother? What does he reveal to Leonato in Act two?

6 By the end of Act two, what adjectives or specific personality traits can you use to describe Leonato?

7 Leonato and his niece have what seems to be a very honest relationship. Describe what the reader discovers about Leonato's desires and Beatrice's desires in regard to a husband in the early parts of the play.

8 How would you describe the interaction between Leonato and Dogberry in Act three Scene 5?

9   In Act four Scene 1, what is Leonato's first reaction to Claudio's accusations?

10   Later in the same act, explain Leonato's anger, frustration, and shock in regard to his daughter's alleged behavior.

Beatrice

1   Describe the first story about Benedick that Beatrice tells the messenger.

2   What is Beatrice's response to the messenger when he tells her that Benedick has performed well in the wars?

3   According to Beatrice, what happened to four of Benedick's wits the last time they met?

4   What are your early impressions of Beatrice? Choose three to four adjectives to use in your answer.

5   Describe the conversation that Beatrice and Benedick have in Act one.

6   Name the three people specifically involved in tricking Beatrice into believing that Benedick is in love with her.

7   Find Beatrice's response to Benedick in Act four when he asks her if she has stayed in Hero's room the previous night.

8   What does Beatrice ask Benedick to do in response to the accusations against her cousin Hero?

9   In Act five Scene 2, Beatrice refuses to kiss Benedick. Find her exact response to his ". . . I will kiss thee" comment.

10   Describe the scene in Act five Scene 4 between Beatrice and Benedick in regard to being married.

Benedick

1   Evaluate Benedick's first statement in the play. What does this say about his personality?

2   By the end of Act one, what are your impressions of Benedick?

3   Is he in favor of marriage early in the play? Why or why not?

4   What does he call Beatrice in Act one Scene 1? What is he implying?

5   When Claudio asks Benedick for his opinion about Hero, what is Benedick's response?

6   Name the three men involved in tricking Benedick into believing that Beatrice loves him.

7   Where is Benedick hiding when he overhears the conversation about Beatrice?

8   When Benedick complains of a toothache, who does he ask to walk with him and what is the implied intent of this walk?

9   What is Benedick's reaction to the accusation directed toward Hero?

10 What does Beatrice ask Benedick to do as revenge for Claudio's accusation?

Claudio

1   Where does Claudio come from and what is his title?

2   What was his first impression of Hero before the war, which he reveals in a conversation with the Prince?

3   How does he feel about Hero in the early stages of the play?

4   How does Claudio describe Hero?

5   Does he seem to be sincere about his feelings in Act one?

6   Don John tells Claudio a lie at the party—what is it about?

7   Who is Claudio's best friend?

8   At the wedding, what is Claudio's response to the Friar's first question?

9   What is Claudio's response when he learns that the accusations against Hero are false?

10   Allegedly, who does Claudio marry at the end of the play?

Don John

1   What does the reader learn about Don John from the first line he speaks?

2   Describe the conversation between Conrade and Don John at the beginning of Act one Scene 3.

3   How does Don John react to Borachio's news?

4   In a brief 2–3 sentence paragraph, describe Don John's personality.

5   From what you know of Don John after the first act, predict what might happen regarding his character.

6   Don John schemes to ruin Claudio's marriage to Hero. What is his reasoning for this deceitful and destructive act?

7   Where does Don John take the Prince and Claudio late that night?

8   Who is Don John's right-hand man?

9   When does Don John escape from Messina?

10   When Don John is captured, what is going on at the time?

Rumors and Innuendos

1   The first rumor that we hear in the play is the story that Antonio tells his brother Leonato. What is the story? Is it accurate?

2   At the end of Act one, Borachio reveals to Don John something that he overheard. Repeat what he tells Don John. Is his story accurate?

3   Innuendos are unpleasant insinuations or accusations. What does Don John insinuate about Claudio and his brother Don Pedro in the early part of the play?

4   What are the accusations that Don John lays upon Hero later in the play?

5   Describe the two intentional and invented rumors played out by various characters to trick Beatrice and Benedick.

The Battle of Wits

Throughout the play, many battles of wits occur with various characters, and most of them include Benedick. Go back through the play and describe in detail the battles of wits in each of the following instances.

- Act one Scene 1—Benedick and Beatrice
- Act two Scene 1—Benedick and Beatrice
- Act two Scene 3—Benedick and Beatrice
- Act three Scene 2—Benedick, Claudio, Prince, Leonato
- Act three Scene 4—Margaret and Beatrice
- Act four Scene 1—Benedick and Beatrice
- Act five Scene 1—Benedick, Prince, Claudio
- Act five Scene 1—Benedick and Margaret
- Act five Scene 2—Benedick and Beatrice
- Act five Scene 4—Benedick, Claudio, Prince
- Act five Scene 5—Benedick and Beatrice

Disguises and Masques

Several events throughout *Much Ado About Nothing* involve disguises or the use of masks. During the Renaissance, "masques" were large parties or balls that required the participants to wear a mask or other disguise. Review the scenes listed below. Describe what is going on in the plot at the time, who is involved in the scene, and where it is set.

- Act two Scene 1
- Act three Scene 3
- Act five Scene 4

Hero's Villain

As you know, Hero is a victim of false accusations. Many characters are involved in carrying out the wrong-doing, including characters are who are not directly involved in the plot itself but play a part in it in some manner. With the list of character names below, describe in detail how they are involved with the plot against Hero and whether or not their actions are a major cause of her downfall. Be thorough.

- Don John
- Borachio
- Conrade
- Margaret
- Claudio
- Prince
- Benedick
- Beatrice
- Friar Francis
- Watchmen
- Leonato
- Antonio

Confusion and Comic Relief

Dogberry, Verges, and other members of the night watch provide much comic relief in the middle of a situation that is quite unpleasant, particularly for Hero. Complete the activities below to help clarify all of this confusion.

- In Act three Scene 3, find the words that Dogberry and/or the watchmen intend to say, but say these instead:

  desartless
  senseless
  comprehend
  vagrom
  tolerable
  vigitant
  recovered
  lechery
  "Masters, never speak, we charge you; let us obey you to go with us."

- In the same act, the watchmen overhear Borachio talking to Conrade about fashion and it's "deformity." The first watchman is confused—explain what HE believes they are talking about.

- In Act three Scene 5, find the words that Dogberry and/or the watchmen intend to say, but say these instead:

  confidence
  decerns
  blunt
  comprehended
  aspicious
  suffigance
  examination
  excommunication

- In Act four Scene 2, find the words that Dogberry and/or the watchmen intend to say, but say these instead:

  dissembly
  exhibition
  eftest
  perjury
  redemption
  opinion'd
  suspect

Love Triumphant

From the beginning of the play to the end of the play, describe the ups and downs of the two intertwining love stories. Make a plot line for each couple, and describe the chronological events from the beginning of the play to the end. Explain the differences in the two love stories.

- Claudio and Hero

- Beatrice and Benedick

Examination Questions

1   Explain what exactly makes this play a comedy.
2   Beatrice and Benedick have become two of Shakespeare's most loved characters. What makes them so likeable?
3   In the early part of the play, Don John makes Claudio believe that the Prince is wooing Hero for himself. Could this be considered an example of foreshadowing? Why or why not?
4   Do you believe that Claudio should be more suspicious of Don John and his accusations against Hero? Explain.
5   When the Prince, Claudio, Benedick, and Don John arrive in Messina, from where have they just come, and what were they doing there?
6   Margaret plays a part in the victimization of Hero. Describe her part in this plot and the depth of her innocence or guilt.
7   Compare and contrast the two couples. How are they different and how are they alike?
8   Give an account of the scene involving the men and their efforts to convince Benedick of Beatrice's love.
9   Give an account of the scene involving the women and their efforts to convince Beatrice of Benedick's love.
10 If the story of Beatrice and Benedick were removed, explain the impact on the plot of this play.
11 Leonato mentions his wife during the play, but she is not a character. Explain the reason(s) why Shakespeare perhaps left her out of the story.
12 What are the advantages and/or disadvantages of the witty banter that continues throughout the play?

13   Borachio brags about his encounter with Margaret, but describe how he defends her at the time of his arrest.

14   The watchmen seem to have a lot of questions for Dogberry and Verges before they are set to take on their positions. Relate some of these questions and how they are answered between Dogberry and Verges.

15   Detail the plan the friar invents to cover Hero's humiliation and shame.

16   What exactly does Claudio agree to near the end of the play when he discovers that he and the Prince have been deceived by Don John?

17   What does Claudio hang on the tomb?

18   Why does Don John leave Messina and what happens to him?

19   Would you agree that Benedick and Beatrice use their wit as a disguise? Explain.

20   Ursula and Antonio are minor characters in the play. Could they be written out of the play or should their characters be left as is?

Fill-in-the-Blank Quiz

1   The play takes place in the city of _____.
2   This city is located in _____.
3   _____ is the name of Hero's father.
4   Beatrice is _____ cousin.
5   Antonio is _____ brother.
6   At the beginning of the play a _____ rides up to the group and delivers a letter.
7   Signior Mountanto is the name that _____ uses to refer to Benedick.
8   Claudio falls in love immediately with _____.
9   _____ is not a man of many words.
10   Conrade and Borachio are _____ companions.
11   The Prince is related to _____.
12   Claudio is _____ related to anyone in the play.
13   In addition to being Beatrice's uncle, _____ seems to be a wealthy man.
14   The character responsible for marrying Claudio and Hero is _____.
15   Margaret is Hero's _____.
16   The constable of Messina is _____.
17   _____ is his partner.
18   _____ is the leader of the watch.
19   _____ devises the story about Hero's alleged death.
20   The play has a _____ ending.

Quotation Quiz

Search the **original** text of the play to finish the partially completed quotations below. (Hint: The quotations are in chronological order beginning in Act one and ending in Act five.)

1 "A victory is twice itself when the achiever brings home . . ."

2 "I wonder that you will still be talking, Signior Benedick, . . ."

3 "God keep your Ladyship still in that mind! so some gentleman or other shall scape . . ."

4 "I thank you. I am not of many words, but . . ."

5 "I would scarce trust myself, though I had sworn the contrary, . . ."

6 "That a woman conceived me, I thank her; that she brought me up, I likewise give . . ."

7 "I had rather be a canker in a hedge than a rose in his grace, and it better fits my blood to be disdain'd of all than to fashion a carriage . . ."

8 "Not till God make men of some other mettle than earth. Would it not grieve a woman to be overmastered with a . . ."

9 "Signior, you are very near my brother in his love. He is enamored on Hero. I pray you dissuade him from her. She is no . . ."

10 "Silence is the perfectest herald of joy. I were but little happy if . . ."

11 "Your silence most offends me, and to be merry best becomes you, for out a' question . . ."

12 "This can be no trick. The conference was sadly borne; they have the truth of this from Hero; they . . ."

13   "O god of love! I know he doth deserve as much as may be yielded to a man; But Nature never fram'd a woman's heart of . . ."

14   "The word is too good to paint out her wickedness. I could say she were worse; think you a worse title, and I . . ."

15   "Why, you speak like an ancient and most quiet watchman, for I cannot see how sleeping should offend; only have a care that your . . ."

16   "Well, masters, we hear our charge. Let us go sit here upon the church bench till two, and . . ."

17   "All this I see, and I see that the fashion wears out more apparel . . ."

18   "Lady, you come hither to be married . . .?"

19   "Oh Fate! take not away thy heavy hand. Death is the fairest cover for her shame that may . . ."

20   "There is some strange misprision . . ."

At last! Shakespeare in Language everyone can understand...

SHAKESPEARE MADE EASY Series

Scene 7

Macbeth's castle. Enter a **sewer** *directing divers servants. Then enter* **Macbeth**.

Macbeth If it were done, when 'tis done, then 'twere well
It were done quickly: if th' assassination
Could trammel up the consequence, and catch,
With his surcease, success; that but this blow
5 Might be the be-all and the end-all here,
But here, upon this bank and shoal of time,
We'd jump the life to come. But in these cases
We still have judgement here: that we but teach
Blood instructions, being taught return
10 To plague th'inventor: this even-handed justice
Commends th'ingredience of our poisoned chalice
To our own lips. He's here in double trust:
First, as I am his kinsman and his subject,
Strong both against the deed: then, as his host,
15 Who should against his murderer shut the door,
Not bear the knife myself. Besides, this Duncan
Hath borne his faculties so meek, hath been
So clear in his great office, that his virtues
Will plead like angels, trumpet-tounged, against
20 The deep damnation of his taking-off;
And pity, like a naked new-born babe,
Striding the blast, or Heaven's cherubin, horsed
Upon the sightless couriers of the air,
Shall blow the horrid deed in every eye,
25 That tears shall drown the wind. I have no spur
To prick the sides of my intent, but only
Vaulting ambition, which o'erleaps itself,
And falls on th'other –

Scene 7

A room in **Macbeth's** *castle. A* **Butler** *and several* **Waiters** *cross, carrying dishes of food. Then* **Macbeth** *enters. He is thinking about the proposed murder of* **King Duncan**.

Macbeth If we could get away with the deed after it's done, then the quicker it were done, the better. If the murder had no consequences, and his death ensured success...If, when I strike the blow, that would be the end of it – here, right here, on this side of eternity – we'd willingly chance the life to come. But usually, we get what's coming to us here on earth. We teach the art of bloodshed, then become the victims of our own lessons. This evenhanded justice makes us swallow our own poison. [*Pause*] Duncan is here on double trust: first, because I'm his kinsman and his subject (both good arguments against the deed); then, because I'm his host, who should protect him from his murderer–not bear the knife. Besides, this Duncan has used his power so gently, he's been so incorruptible his great office, that his virtues will plead like angels, their tongues trumpeting the damnable horror of his murder. And pity, like a naked newborn babe or Heaven's avenging angels riding the winds, will cry the deed to everyone so that tears will blind the eye. I've nothing to spur me on but high-leaping ambition, which can often bring about one's downfall.

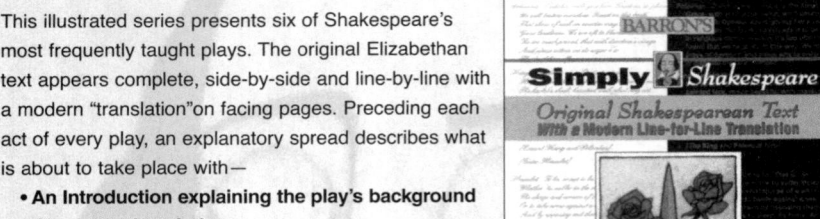
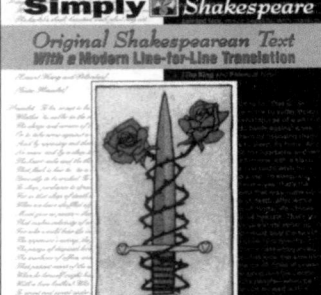